The Bideford, Westward Ho! & Appledore Railway

Rod Garner

©Kestrel Railway Books and Rod Garner 2008

Kestrel Railway Books
PO Box 269
SOUTHAMPTON
SO30 4XR

www.kestrelrailwaybooks.co.uk

All rights reserved.

No part of this publication may be reproduced, stored in a retrieval system, transmitted in any form or by any means, electronic, mechanical, or photocopied, recorded or otherwise, without the consent of the publisher in writing.

Printed by the Amadeus Press

ISBN 978-1-905505-09-8

Northamptonshire Libraries

Front cover: Looking up the road from the beach towards the station at Westward Ho!.
(Tom Bartlett Postcard Collection)

Back cover: Bideford Quay in about 1906. A train waits quietly on the Quay road before departure.
(Tom Bartlett Postcard Collection)

Contents

Acknowledgments and Bibliography iv

Preface v

Chapter 1.	**Historical Background**	**1**
	History and Geography	1
	Railway Development in North Devon	10
Chapter 2.	**Plans are Laid**	**17**
	Preliminary Steps	17
	The Act is Passed	21
	Construction	28
	Battle Lines are Drawn	30
	Inspection and Approval	40
Chapter 3.	**To Westward Ho! and Beyond**	**43**
	The Inspector Returns	43
	Problems at the Quay	45
	B.E.T Rally Round	53
Chapter 4.	**Operation and Extension**	**57**
	On to Appledore	57
	Operation and Obstruction	62
	A Journey Down the Line	72
Chapter 5.	**Rolling Stock and Infrastructure**	**81**
	Locomotives	81
	Coaching Stock	87
	Goods Wagons	89
	Signalling	90
	Civil Engineering Works	94
	Track	94
Chapter 6.	**The Final Years**	**95**
	Traffic, Timetables and Fares	95
	Staff	99
	Twilight	100

Appendix A. The Bideford, Clovelly & Hartland proposals 111

Appendix B. Accidents and Incidents 113

Appendix C. The Railway Inspectorate 114

Dedication

~ For Anita ~

Acknowledgments

I set out on my researches for this book anticipating a round of checking out sources of already published material and photographs, but I soon discovered that there was more to the story than I had previously thought. I have used my theory of lateral thinking to good effect in tracing material, and many people have gone out of their way to help me in my quest and they are acknowledged here. If I have missed anyone from this list it is entirely unintentional and I can only apologize most profusely.

The first major source of material I discovered was the Bideford Community Archive in Northam and I cannot thank Pat Slade and Bob Elliott enough for their guidance and assistance over many weeks trawling through back numbers of the *Bideford Gazette*. The amount of detail recorded in the pages of the *Gazette* is quite incredible and this provides a major thread of my story. Rose Arno and her colleagues at Bideford Library were incredibly generous in allowing me access to some really interesting archive photographs.

To Chris Leigh goes my sincere thanks for so generously loaning me his collection of photographs and for guidance in my researches. Don Townsley has also been most generous in providing a mouth-watering amount of information on the motive power front. Roger Griffiths generously loaned me much original research material. As always everyone at the North Devon Record office in Barnstaple has been most helpful, as has Lyn Williams at the Beaford Archive. Sincere thanks to Ian Pringle for access to his superb railway ticket collection. Roger Benton of the Tramway Museum at Crich has provided some amazing and interesting material for which I am most grateful. Carol Morgan of the Institution of Civil Engineers provided some interesting background to J.T. Jervis the line's engineer. Staff at the National Archive at Kew were most helpful and unearthed a surprisingly vast amount of material for me to devour.

Thanks also to Tom Bartlett, Rob Dark, Clive Fairchild, Felton Vowler, Ian Dinmore, Maureen Richards and Marilyn Hughes of the Westward Ho! History Group, The Lens of Sutton Association, Roger Carpenter, the Post Office archives, House of Lords archive, and Martin Dowding for producing some excellent maps and drawings.

Bibliography

To attempt to list all the material I have consulted is difficult, but the following are the major sources I have used:

The Bideford, Westward Ho! & Appledore Railway, Stanley Jenkins
The Bideford, Westward Ho! & Appledore Railway, Douglas Stuckey
The Bideford, Westward Ho! and Appledore Railway (1901–1917), J.& J. Baxter
Old Bideford & District, Muriel Goaman
Minor Railways of England and their Locomotives, George Woodcock
Industrial Locomotives of South Western England, Industrial Railway Society
Regional History of the Railways of Great Britain – Volume 1 – The West Country, David St John Thomas
The Railways of Devon, Martin Smith
College project, Roger Griffiths
Steam Days – July 1992, article by Chris Leigh
Copies of the relevant Acts and Light Railway Orders
Railway Magazine, various editions

Preface

When it was first suggested to me that the Bideford, Westward Ho! & Appledore Railway was a good subject for my attention, I was not convinced. There were already two or three books on the subject – albeit out of print – and it had been touched upon in various other publications over the years. However, my curiosity soon got the better of me and I started digging in local archives. In a short space of time I had discovered much that was previously unknown to me, and which I had not seen in print before; I was hooked!

The story of the Bideford, Westward Ho! & Appledore line is far from the traditional tale of the construction of a new railway. It does have many of the usual ingredients: difficulties in raising capital and buying land, protracted negotiations regarding Parliamentary approval and contractor troubles. Here however, we have a small group of local entrepreneurs with the drive and determination to create not just a railway, but a railway to serve a new town and harbour they also planned to build. In spite of considerable local support there was also bitter opposition from the Council which dogged the line throughout its short life. A change of gauge was also thrown in to add fuel to the fire of opposition. The new railway was also completely isolated from the rest of the system, although as we shall see that was far from the original idea. Had all the various parts of the overall scheme originally envisaged by its promoters been brought to fruition, the history of the area might have been very different, and railway travel from London to Westward Ho!, Appledore and beyond might have been possible even today.

Originally planned and built as a normal railway, the first part of the line was actually a street tramway before it ventured out into the countryside as a normal railway. The extension however was built under a Light Railway Order and the whole line was eventually operated under Light Railway Regulations. In spite of this, the word "Light" never appeared in the title.

It has been a great adventure researching this little line and gradually uncovering the story of its struggle for life and existence, and part of that pleasure has been the involvement with the people who have helped me along the way. It is true to say that without them this work would not have been possible. Their names are mentioned in the Acknowledgement section as a small thank you to them.

Rod Garner
Torrington
March 2008

A nicely posed view of a two coach train on the Quay loop line. The locomotive is either "Grenville" or "Kingsley". (Chris Leigh Collection)

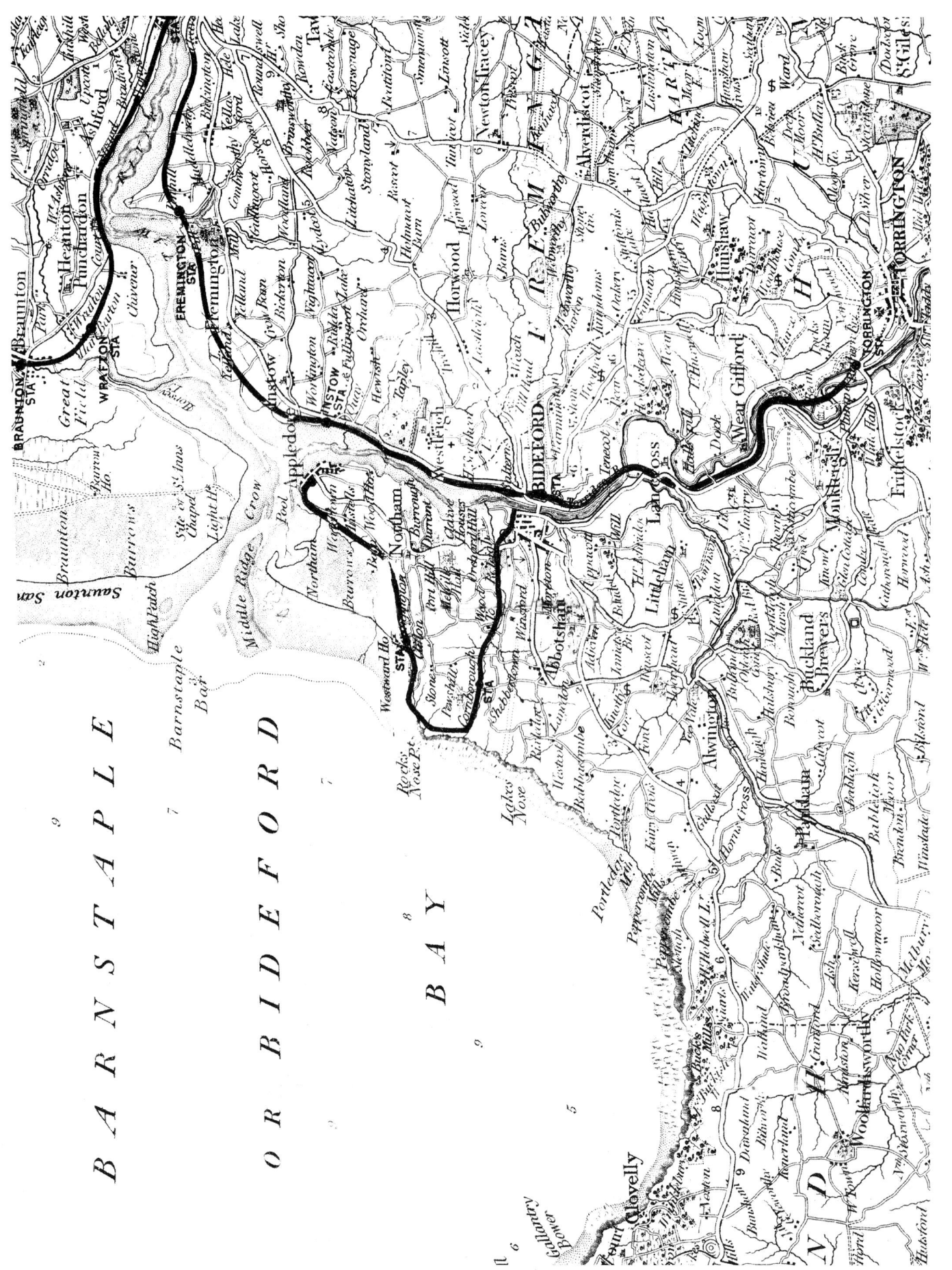

Chapter 1

Historical Background

History and Geography

Devon is often rightly called "Glorious Devon" and the north of the county is no exception to this description. It is an area of great contrasts: beautiful rolling countryside studded with shady woodland, picturesque market towns, the wild beauty of western Exmoor, spectacular cliff top scenery inset with wide sandy beaches, steep wooded valleys running down to tiny harbours, and a wide estuary where the Taw and Torridge rivers meet and run together into Bideford Bay.

The traditional employment for most of the men-folk in North Devon in earlier days was either working the land as farmers, or the sea as fishermen. The fishermen built their own boats, usually at the quay or harbour they sailed from, and shipbuilding flourished, largely around the various estuaries. These early fishermen eventually ventured further afield becoming some of Britain's earliest maritime merchants trading goods round the southwest peninsular and across the Bristol Channel to South Wales, eventually reaching as far as America, Africa and the Indies.

The seas off this north coast are extremely treacherous with the Atlantic Ocean sweeping past the rock-strewn cliffs and up the Bristol Channel. The tidal range here is the second highest in the world creating strong and unpredictable currents, and in the days of sail the north Devon coast was considered to be one of the most dangerous places on the high seas. It was at Appledore that one of the earliest purpose-built lifeboats, the *Volunteer*, was stationed in 1825. Little surprise then, that the likes of Drake, Raleigh and Grenville were such proficient seamen, having learnt their craft off the Devon coasts.

The southwest has always produced men of great drive, tenacity and imagination; fashioned by the climate and the environment. Men who became engineers, inventors, businessmen, as well as sailors, and who played an important part in the development of railways throughout the world in the nineteenth century. In past times, few people travelled far from where they lived and North Devon was little known to outsiders. South Devon had become a Mecca for those seeking the pleasures of the seaside in the mid to late eighteenth century but it was almost one hundred years later

Old Bideford Bridge in about 1863. This view shows four adjacent public houses on the Quay: The Steam Packet & Railway Hotel, The Newfoundland (now the Rose of Torridge, named after the girl Rose Salterne in Kingsley's novel "Westward Ho!"), The Kings Arms and the Three Tuns Inn. (Bideford Library)

THE BIDEFORD, WESTWARD HO! & APPLEDORE RAILWAY

An undated, high-vantage view of Bideford from the south, looking downstream. (Bideford Library)

before the Victorians discovered the charms of North Devon, and with the arrival of the railway – firstly to Barnstaple, then Bideford, Ilfracombe and Lynton – tourism boomed. Visitors flocked to the area and were conveyed from the railway stations and around the area by horse drawn coaches.

However, we are concerned here with only a small slice of North Devon being the peninsula of land running north from the port of Bideford up between the Torridge estuary and Bideford Bay. Travelling down the Torridge towards the sea from Bideford we pass by Northam, Burrough and thence to Appledore. Turning north-westerly we cross the bleak expanse of Northam Burrows and turn south along the high pebble ridge, make a dog-leg to the west and then down south-westerly past Rock Nose Point to Cornborough Cliffs. Notice that there is no mention in that description of the town of Westward Ho! for at the time this story begins it did not exist. It is this relatively small tract of land that is the setting for the rather strange story of the Bideford, Westward Ho! & Appledore Railway.

"All who have travelled through the delicious scenery of North Devon must needs know the little white town of Bideford, which slopes upwards from its broad tide-river paved with yellow sands, and many-arched old bridge where salmon wait for autumn floods, toward the pleasant upland on the west. Above the town the hills close in, cushioned with deep oak woods, through which juts here and there a crag of fern-fringed slate. Below they lower, and open more and more in softly rounded knolls, and fertile squares of red and green, till they sink into the wide expanse of hazy flats, rich salt-marshes, and rolling sand-hills, where Torridge joins her sister Taw, and both together flow quietly toward the broad surges of the bar, and the everlasting thunder of the long Atlantic swell. Pleasantly the old town stands there, beneath its soft Italian sky, fanned day and night by the fresh ocean breeze, which forbids alike the keen winter frosts, and the fierce thunder heats of the midland. Pleasantly it has stood there for now, perhaps, eight hundred years since the first Grenville, cousin of the Conqueror, returning from the conquest of South Wales, drew round him trusty Saxon serfs, and free Norse rovers with their golden curls, and dark Silurian Britons from the Swansea shore, and all the mingled blood which still gives to the seaward folk of the next county their strength and intellect, and, even in these levelling days, their peculiar beauty of face and form."

So begins Charles Kingsley's famous novel *Westward Ho!* and his description of Bideford still stands well today, although the buildings are somewhat more multicoloured than in his time. Kingsley was very fond of this area and in recognition of the locals' regard for him they erected a statue in his honour in 1906, which still graces the edge of the park and looks up the Quay towards that "many-arched old bridge". It is thought that the 24-arch bridge – which links Bideford to its neighbour East-the-Water – dates back to a thirteenth century wooden structure just downstream from an earlier ford over the river. When Bideford seafarers such as Sir Richard Grenville were active on the high seas, Bideford was the country's third largest port and it was Grenville who persuaded Elizabeth I to grant the town its royal charter in 1573. Grenville's colonisation of Carolina and Virginia generated a flow of trade across the Atlantic guaranteeing Bideford's position as a major trading port. This lasted until the colonies broke away and declared independence. In 1588, Bideford sent merchant ships of 200 and 300 tons to assist the fleet in fighting the Armada. Daniel Defoe (1660-1731) wrote:

HISTORICAL BACKGROUND

Bridge Buildings and the Quay seen from East-the-Water. (Bideford Library)

"Biddiford is a pleasant, clean, well-built town. The more ancient street, which lies next the river, is very pleasant, where is the bridge, a very noble quay and the custom house."

Apart from a range of general merchandise, ball clay from the Peters Marland clay fields was exported from here over the years, and as early as 1654-55, William and Jasper Greening – both ships' masters – were carrying tobacco-pipe clay to Gloucester and further afield. Potteries were active in the town between about 1668 and 1896. The Quay on the west bank of the river was originally much smaller than it is today having been extended and widened several times over the years. At the site of the Technical School the Pill ran inland, becoming the Kenwith Stream, and was crossed by an old causeway. In 1825 work began to drain the marshy land to the north of the River and the reclaimed land eventually became Victoria Park. In 1844 a bridge was built over the Pill, and the Quay itself was widened in 1889/1890 and trees planted along a newly created promenade in 1891. Quays run along both sides of the river, downstream from the bridge, although the west quay is currently the most used. Clay is still loaded on ships from Bideford Quay, regrettably arriving from the clay works in huge lorries.

The "Marquis of Lorne" alongside the Quay. She was a screw-driven, iron-built ship, and plied her trade between Bideford and Bristol until about 1894. She replaced the "Neath Abbey", which had been lost on rocks near Nash Point in South Wales in 1867. The slipway shown here disappeared when the Quay was widened in 1889. (Bideford Library)

THE BIDEFORD, WESTWARD HO! & APPLEDORE RAILWAY

The Quay before widening, probably in about 1888 or 1889. This view shows Pickford's block of buildings and Trewin's Chain Stores on the corner of King Street. Note the unmade road. (Bideford Library)

The Quay after the widening and before the trees were planted along the promenade. The Kings Arms can be seen in the background on the left. (Bideford Library)

HISTORICAL BACKGROUND

A delightfully rural view near Appledore, showing the remoteness of the area. (Beaford Archive)

Appledore Quay soon after 1900. (Tom Bartlett Postcard Collection)

The parish of Northam included the village of that name as well as Appledore and latterly, Westward Ho! Burrough lies just outside Northam village and was the home of the sixteenth century explorers and navigators, Stephen and William Burrough (or Borough). It was here that Charles Kingsley set his story of Westward Ho! Unfortunately the views from the town today are spoiled by modern "developments".

The little port of Appledore dates back to at least the fourteenth century and was of importance as being the first place where ships could berth after coming in over Bideford bar. It increased in importance as Bideford prospered and a shipbuilding industry grew up which is still active today. Westward Ho! as a place and name did not exist at all until Kingsley's book was published in 1855 and the land it now occupies was at this time an unspoilt panorama of wide sweeping beach and uninhabited sandy scrub land which was merely the end of the long pebble ridge forming the western edge of Northam Burrows.

South Western Railway newspaper advertisement for horse drawn coaches to Clovelly and Bude, from June 1889.

Travelling much further west along the coast we come to Clovelly and Hartland, and whilst these places do not figure in the main story, they do form part of the initial stirrings of the venture. Clovelly is a small village perched precariously on either side of a very steep pebbled roadway which runs down to a little harbour. Some of the buildings reputedly date from Tudor times and the very nature of the site has prevented it being extended or expanded, and it remains today very much as it has been for hundreds of years. Herring was the most important catch off these coasts and at one time some 60 – 70 boats worked out of Clovelly. By 1840 the three fishing ports of Clovelly, Barnstaple and Appledore together were ranked the third largest in the country.

Charles Kingsley loved this part of Devon, spending much time here, mainly recuperating from illnesses, and in August 1849 wrote to his wife from Appledore: "I feel myself much better. The coast down here looked more lovely than ever; the green fern and purple heather have enriched the colouring since the spring; showers succeeded by gleams of sun, give a wonderful freshness and delicacy to all the tints."

Further west along the coast is Hartland Point, where the coast turns sharply south, with the village of Hartland lying

Clovelly's High Street climbing up the hillside from the harbour. (Author's Collection)

HISTORICAL BACKGROUND

An early view of Westward Ho! from Kipling Tors. The desolate nature of the area at this time can be appreciated from this view. (Beaford Archive)

just a few miles inland. Hartland Quay is a couple of miles further down the coast. The harbour was financed by Sir Francis Drake, Sir Walter Raleigh and Sir John Hawkins in the sixteenth century as a refuge for their fellow mariners from the storms which rage round this promontory. It fell into disuse at the end of the nineteenth century and its remains are now barely discernible. The whole region was quite desolate and sparsely inhabited until the late nineteenth century and today one can still travel for miles without seeing much in the way of human presence.

Several enterprising local landowners were keen to develop the barren land near Northam Burrows into a fashionable resort to compete with towns like Ilfracombe and Torquay. The most influential of these was Captain George Mill Frederick Molesworth, J.P., R.N. (retired) of North Down House, Strand, Bideford. (North Down House is reputedly where Kingsley wrote much of his famous novel.) Molesworth was a notable personality and landowner in the area and well acquainted with what was going on in the world at large and in particular with regard to railways.

On 25th March 1863, the Northam Burrows (North Devon) Hotel & Villa Building Company was floated for erection of grand hotels and villas in the area, underlining their desire to develop the land, and a railway link was felt to be vital. In February 1864, the Countess of Portsmouth laid the foundation stone of the Royal Hotel. Charles Kingsley was invited to perform the opening ceremony. He declined at first, being dismayed at the thought of development spoiling the area, but was persuaded to change his mind when the hotel's name was changed to the Westward Ho! Hotel after the success of his novel, published in 1855. The hotel boasted 33 luxury bedrooms and opened for business in June 1865. The following year, a large villa – Golden Bay Court – was opened close by as an annexe to the hotel. The Hotel company soon changed its name to the Westward Ho! Hotel and Villa Company Limited. A year earlier, in 1863, the North Devon and West of England Golf Club was founded; only the second course south of the border, and three years later the Prince of Wales joined the Club. On 31st October 1867 a contract concluded for the erection of 12 semi-detached villas on the slope facing the bay at what was thenceforth known as Westward Ho!

THE BIDEFORD, WESTWARD HO! & APPLEDORE RAILWAY

The Westward Ho! Hotel. (Beaford Archive)

A view of Westward Ho!, showing some of the new development. (Beaford Archive)

HISTORICAL BACKGROUND

Westward Ho! pier, nearing completion in about 1870. It is hardly surprising that the pier succumbed to the elements, given the light nature of the construction.
(Tom Bartlett Postcard Collection)

In 1868 the Rev Edward Dansey, Rural Dean of Hartland, laid the foundation stone for a new church in the fast developing new settlement. The Dean had offered stones from his quarry for the new church, which was estimated to cost almost £2,000, and it was opened by the Bishop of Exeter on 24th March 1870. As a sign of the growing importance of the town, the Post Master General authorised a Post Office at Westward Ho! in 1870 and it was reported that "Miss Manley was to open the office in one of the newly taken shops".

According to *Morris's Directory* for 1870, "The first idea was simply to build an hotel and a few villas, but so extremely bracing and pure was the air found to be, and so conducive to health for persons suffering from chest and other complaints, that several eminent medical men sent their patients, and at their suggestion large houses, with every comfort, were built, and this led to the erection of shops and rows of terraces, which now adorn this beautiful watering place."

Publication of the novel *Lorna Doone* by R.D. Blackmore in 1869 added to the attraction of the area for the curious tourist, and the next year the Northam Burrows Promenade and Landing Pier Company was established to build a pier at Westward Ho! and work started on 30th June on a 600ft long structure. Mr C.S. Inman was resident engineer for the firm of Gooch who had previously built Bognor Regis pier. The story of the ceremony of laying the first plank is related later in this chapter. The pier was first open to the public in 1871, whilst still uncompleted, but in October that year, the end was damaged by severe gales. The contract for a new, but much shorter 150ft long pier was re-let to W. & J. Abbott of Bideford. Work started on 4th July 1872 and the completed pier was opened on 24th July 1873. The structure had two pavilions and a "turnaround" at the end for the pony drawn carriages.

On 10th July 1875 the Grand Nassau Baths were opened with a "monster picnic" on the Pier. Captain Webb, who was to be the first man to swim the English Channel 6 weeks later, was present and gave a display.

Ill luck, or perhaps a poor design also dogged the second attempt at pier building. Another severe storm during the winter of 1880 caused fatal damage and the pier was dismantled in the spring of 1881. The remains of some of the supporting stanchions can still be seen at low tide.

THE BIDEFORD, WESTWARD HO! & APPLEDORE RAILWAY

Railway Development in North Devon

Even as early as the 1830s, the people of North Devon had realised the importance railways would play in the future, and had commissioned a survey for a railway from Bideford to Okehampton through Torrington. The idea behind this proposal was to link Bideford with the central and southern parts of the county and encourage the development of manufacturing in the county and facilitate the movement of goods from Bristol and South Wales. At that time goods were shipped from the ports of north Devon, round Lands End, to those in the south, which added greatly to journey times and costs. Devon roads were still primitive and incapable of carrying much weight of traffic even when the roads were dry.

The Bideford to Okehampton survey never came to fruition and the railways were late in coming to North Devon, the main protagonists having been happy to pass by on their squabbling way further westwards. The Great Western Railway, with the Bristol & Exeter, had opened from London Paddington to Exeter as early as 1844. It was some ten years later that the London & South Western's Exeter to Barnstaple line was opened in 1854, with the extension to Bideford opening the following year. Not until 1860 did the LSWR reach Exeter from the east thus completing their through route to London. It was not until 1874 that the Great Western branch from Taunton was fully operational to Barnstaple, thus opening up access to and from Somerset.

Almost before the first train had entered Bideford, there was tremendous local pressure for the line to be extended, especially to provide a better link with the south and to open up that area still not served by the railway. This pressure was especially vociferous in Torrington, where a meeting on the subject at the Town Hall was reported in the *Bideford Weekly Gazette* of 22nd October 1861.

On 7th April 1863, the *Bideford Weekly Gazette* carried a lengthy article headed "The Railway and the Harbour", which complained about the railway facilities in the town, bemoaning the fact that the station was a mile from the town

The offices and yard of W. Pridham & Son. Pridham operated a large fleet of horse-drawn coaches and wagons in north Devon and were agents for the LSWR. (Bideford Library)

HISTORICAL BACKGROUND

A nice view over the LSWR goods yard, looking across the river towards the Quay. This was formerly Cross Parks station – the broad gauge terminus. It became the goods station when the Torrington extension line opened in 1872. The main line to the new station passes under the bridge and can just be seen in the lower left-hand corner of the photograph. (Beaford Archive)

centre over the river at Cross Parks. The article went on to accuse the railway companies – the London & South Western in particular – of complacency as far as the north of the county was concerned, in not planning extensions southwards to Torrington and Holsworthy and links with the railway network in the south. A new station should be built in Bideford, the article continued, and lines extended to Torrington and Holsworthy, with a branch to Appledore. The silt in the harbour should also be cleaned out so that the port of Bideford could reclaim her title of "Queen of the West".

In Christmas week that year the paper reported that a meeting was to be held in the town to press for the provision of a new station. It was also reported that the LSWR were discussing improvements to the existing station facilities. A further meeting in Bideford in February 1865 discussed ways of opening up communication with Torrington, Plymouth and the west of Cornwall. Eventually, in spite of reluctance on the part of the LSWR, the Torrington Extension Railway was authorised by Parliament on 6th June 1865. The line was to be operated by the LSWR as a standard gauge extension from Bideford. The LSWR's intentions were soon apparent as they did little work on the new line apart from marking out the line and deviations, and with capital difficult to raise in the post "mania" years, they twice attempted to have the Act annulled.

In 1866 a Bill was presented to Parliament for the Bideford, Appledore & Westward Ho! Railway. This proposed construction of a two mile long line from Bideford to Appledore (Railway number 1) with a branch of four miles off the main line to Westward Ho! (Railway number 2). The Bill passed into law on 16th July 1866 with provision for a two year construction period and an authorised capital of £60,000.

Acquisition of the land for the project proved problematic and in 1868 the company applied to Parliament for an extension of time to allow compulsory purchase of some of the land needed, and to raise all the capital required. The application was granted, extending the date for land acquisition to 26th July 1870 and for completion of the line to 26th July 1871.

The matter was still not resolved by 1870, for on 28th June 1870 – almost four years after the Act came into force and only a month before the statutory time ran out – the *Bideford Weekly Gazette* reported that "a movement has been set on foot for carrying out the proposed railway from Bideford to Westward Ho!" and a meeting of landowners and

THE BIDEFORD, WESTWARD HO! & APPLEDORE RAILWAY

A ground level view of the bridge. This view shows the bridge after the rebuilding of 1864. It was rebuilt again in 1925. (Bideford Library)

proprietors of the Westward Ho! estate had been held at the Royal Hotel, when "plans of the proposed scheme were approved, and several persons offered to give the necessary land and otherwise assist in the undertaking". Several landowners offered to give land either free or at "nominal charge". The seemingly statutory luncheon was taken afterwards and the article stated, "In the event of the land question being settled, it is expected that the line will shortly commence and that it will be finished by the end of May next year." Six stations were to be provided: near the Quay at Bideford, at Cliff House, Bidna Knapp, Burrows Road, Appledore and Westward Ho!

How the promoters had decided on the contractor for the venture is not recorded, but one Edward Humphries was appointed to carry out the work and apparently at his own expense, up to £80,000. Presumably he was to be paid by way of share or debenture issues, as was often the case at that time. Humphries was at this stage the contractor on the section of the Teign Valley line from Jews Bridge (Heathfield) on the Moretonhampstead branch, as far as Ashton on the way back to Exeter. He had taken the contract over in September 1869 from Richard Walker who had had various problems with his employers. Humphries' contract with the Teign Valley was for £50,000 payable by way of £45,000 in debenture stock and £5,000 in ordinary stock. Work apparently went quite well on this job until early in July 1870, when work stopped and it was discovered that Humphries was in financial difficulties. Whether these were of his own making, or brought about by lack of payment for work done, or both is unclear. However at the precise time he was getting into severe trouble on the Teign Valley line, Humphries was appointed to build the Bideford, Appledore & Westward Ho! line.

Whilst all this railway activity, or in truth inactivity, was going on, plans for the development of the area now called Westward Ho! were actually bearing fruit. The Westward Ho! Promenade and Landing Pier Company was about to start work on their new pier and it was decided by the local worthies that a dual ceremony would be held to cut the first sod of the new railway and nail the first plank of the new pier. Accordingly, the *Bideford Weekly Gazette* of 2nd August 1870 carried an enthusiastic article about the planned proceedings, which were to take place two days later, on Thursday, 4th August 1870. A grand occasion was planned

HISTORICAL BACKGROUND

> **THE PIER AND RAILWAY**
> AT
> **WESTWARD HO!**
>
> THE FIRST SOD for the BIDEFORD, APPLEDORE, and WESTWARD HO! RAILWAY will be Cut on THURSDAY, the 4th of August next, by
>
> **MISS NORTHCOTE,**
>
> After which the FIRST DECK PLANK of the PIER will be nailed by
>
> **MRS. MOORE-STEVENS,**
>
> Wife of the High Sheriff of the County. The Ceremony will commence at half-past 1 o'clock. A Large
>
> **PUBLIC DINNER**
>
> Consisting of a Cold Collation, will be provided at 3 o'Clock, Tickets 3s. 6d. each.
>
> In the Evening, by particular desire, there will be a
>
> **PUBLIC BALL**
>
> At the Bath House, under the patronage of Lady Northcote, tickets for which, including Refreshments may be obtained at the Royal Hotel, Westward Ho! or of Mr. Griffiths, Stationer, High-street, Bideford, at 5s. each.
>
> STEWARDS:
> J. C. MOORE-STEVENS, Esq., High Sheriff of the County,
> Sir STAFFORD NORTHCOTE, Bart., M.P.,
> J. R. PINE-COFFIN, Esq.
> Lieut.-Colonel HUTCHINSON.
> A. B. WREN, Esq.
> PAUL WILMOT, Esq,
> C. W. HOLE, Esq.,
>
> **WESTWARD HO! BALL,**
> **THURSDAY EVENING, AUGUST 4th, 1870.**
>
> Admittance by Ticket
> at the Bath Room.
> A Demi Toilette Dress.

and the same issue of the paper had a large advertisement for the celebrations with details of tickets for the dinner and ball.

It must have been quite an event, and Miss Northcote – Sir Stafford Northcote's daughter – was presented with a "handsome silver mounted wheelbarrow and spade" for her efforts on the day. Humphries apparently ordered the gift from London at a cost of 80 guineas (£84) but unfortunately failed to pay for it! Humphries owed the West of England & South Wales Bank some £400 and on 27th August the plant he was using on the Teign Valley contract, which was in his works yard at Chudleigh Bridge, was auctioned off. On the Monday morning the purchasers of the plant arrived to find the yard barricaded by angry navvies and their womenfolk who had not been paid for some time.

The *Bideford Weekly Gazette* of 6th September 1870 opened its article on the matter, "It appears that the recent ceremony with respect to cutting the first sod was a perfect farce". The rest of the article reported the matter in a factual manner, but two weeks later, having discovered the true state of the situation, had more to say on the matter. Reminding its readers of the events of the great day, it continued, "We are aware that for what has transpired those who took part in the ceremony are not responsible, but it was not entirely unforeseen, and we are therefore inclined to think that the farce might have been prevented had the proper enquiries been made." The article continues to state that work will continue with new backing. It concluded by hoping that the wheelbarrow and spade would be exhibited in a local shop window with the inscription "Respectfully Declined".

At the end of September, Humphries' case came up in the Bankruptcy Court and after several hearings, Trustees in Bankruptcy were appointed and sold off his remaining assets. It is believed that Humphries died soon afterwards: a sad end to a sorry tale.

An interesting article appeared in the *Bideford Weekly Gazette* on 8th June 1870 regarding "the proposed railway bridge across the Torridge". This short piece referred to the discussion over the £5 fee apparently charged by the Borough Surveyor for producing a plan. The Town Council felt he should not be charging for this sort of work as they deemed it part of his normal duties. No other details are given, but the *Bideford Weekly Gazette* of 16th May 1871 explains the matter further. An article reported the previous day's council meeting, at which the LSWR were yet again berated for not opening a new station in Bideford. It continued reporting that Captain Molesworth had applied for permission to build a "swing railway bridge across the Torridge for a through route to Appledore and Westward Ho! A dock company as well as a railway company was hinted at."

The matter was referred to a meeting the following week. At this later meeting held on 5th June, a plan of the project was produced showing the proposed bridge "below the existing long bridge with a wharf and docks in connection therewith, for a direct railway route to Westward Ho!" Captain Molesworth advised that, "a party of capitalists were (sic) prepared to take the matter in hand, and that the railway company were disposed to regard it favourably". Several councillors were against the plans as "considered to be fatal to the best interests of the town, and likely to interfere considerably with the navigation of the river". After some discussion, the matter was left unresolved.

At a further special meeting on 3rd July, the matter was again considered by the council. This time there was good support for Molesworth's plans. The Mayor however, on behalf of himself and others, objected saying "he did not see why the river should be interfered with merely for the purpose of accommodating a few tourists and two or three residents at Westward Ho!" On a vote, however, the motion in support of the plans was carried by 8 votes to 5. In the light of future developments, the Mayor's comment can be seen as a portent of things to come as far as relations between

THE BIDEFORD, WESTWARD HO! & APPLEDORE RAILWAY

the Council and future railways were concerned.

In the meantime, in 1869, and in the face of strenuous support for the project locally, the LSWR were forced to accept the inevitable as far as the Torrington Extension Railway was concerned, and Parliamentary extension of time for completion was granted. Work began in May 1870 with W.R. Galbraith, the Company's chief engineer, in charge and James Taylor, one of their regular contractors, responsible for the actual construction. Provision of a new station in Bideford at East-the-Water at the end of Bideford long bridge was included in the extension, with the old broad gauge station at Cross Parks being retained for goods traffic.

By February 1871 work was well advanced with the tunnel and viaduct at Landcross being the major works still to be completed. Lt. Col. Yolland of the Board of Trade carried out an inspection on 7th June 1872 and approved the opening of the new station at Bideford, but refused to sanction opening of the rest of the line due to the incompleteness of the works. On his return visit on 12th July, he found matters virtually complete, and his report of the following day noted that only the installation of a crossover at the end of the Torrington platforms was required. He also made a suggestion regarding a catch point off the turntable and shed road. The required work was put in hand immediately and completed early the following week, opening taking place on the following Thursday, 18th July 1872.

A little over a year later, on 1st November 1873 to be exact, the Great Western Railway opened its new broad gauge line from Taunton into a new terminus in Barnstaple, some distance from the LSWR station. The line was "narrowed" in May 1881 and later a connecting spur was laid to what by then had become Barnstaple Junction Station with the opening of the branch line to Ilfracombe in 1884. This spur was opened on 1st June 1887 and allowed through running of GWR trains to Ilfracombe.

As an aside, a report in the *Gazette* noted that a meeting had been held in Appledore on 1st April 1876 to consider proposals for a steam ferry to operate across the estuary from Appledore to Instow. The good Captain Molesworth was present at the meeting, but nothing further appears to have been reported of this idea, although a ferry or some sort did operate over this stretch of the river.

A tentative step in further railway expansion in the area

A high-level view of Bideford LSWR station (actually situated in East-the-Water) looking over the bridge towards the Quay. The train is composed of LSWR 6-wheel coaches. (Beaford Archive)

HISTORICAL BACKGROUND

was the opening on 1st January 1881 of the 3ft gauge Torrington & Marland Light Railway, from the LSWR's station at Torrington to the clay works at Peters Marland. Whilst this assisted the clay company in moving its products and was of some use locally, it did nothing to fill the need for connections to the south and west. In its article of 10th February 1881, announcing the official opening of the Marland line, the *Bideford Weekly Gazette* voiced the opinion that "hopes are entertained too that at no distant date a similar line of railway may connect Bideford with Westward Ho! and Barnstaple with Lynton".

Stirrings for a proper extension of the railway south from Torrington were soon heard and proposals for a line to Launceston were voiced in an article in the *Bideford Weekly Gazette* of 5th July 1881. Some two months later a letter from "LOOKER-ON" made his (or her?) views known in suggesting that, whilst a railway westwards along the coast towards Clovelly may be fine for tourists, more thought should be given to lines which "would **pay** for the construction of the line". The letter continues by rather belittling the port of Bideford, "now only a 'creek' of the port of Barnstaple" and continues: "You must sweep away the cobwebs which seem to be obscuring the vision of some of our friends. We must open up, by the most direct route possible, the country to the south-west." The letter concludes that the route "should sweep round to Hatherleigh, thence via Halwill to Launceston".

Subsequent events show that the writer's suggestions came to be realised, but whilst Halwill and Launceston were connected by 1886, it was not until 1925 that the route from Torrington to Halwill was built. Matters appeared to simmer quietly for a while until a letter from "PROGRESS" appeared in the *Bideford Weekly Gazette* of 27th November 1883. In it he questions what has happened on the matter of further railway development in the preceding two years, and notes that work on the Halwill to Launceston link was about to start. "What of Torrington to Halwill?" he asks. No response appears to have been forthcoming.

Rails pushed up through Halwill Junction to Holsworthy in 1879, but the good people of Bideford were still unhappy with the situation and an editorial in the *Bideford Weekly Gazette* of 13th August 1889 reports a decision by the council at the previous evening's meeting to invite the GWR to extend to Bideford. This, it states, is "in consequence of the continued apathy of the L. & S. W. R. Company" in not extending their facilities in the town. Feeling against the LSWR was clearly running strong. The following week's issue of the *Gazette* however carried a letter from "A NEW RESIDENT" warning of the dangers of upsetting the LSWR. He suggests that the GWR may well behave exactly the same way if they had the monopoly and that the town would do well to "keep in the good graces of L. & S. W. R. Co., who are on the whole serving the town well. The power of a Railway Co. for the good or ill of a town on their system is very great, and friends are far better than enemies."

Presumably no action resulted on this and again this matter simmered quietly until the *Gazette* raises it again on 14th June 1892, again reporting a council meeting. A motion was passed again calling upon the GWR to extend to Bideford. An amendment suggesting the LSWR be pressed to make "better arrangements" was defeated. How the motion went down with the powers that be in Paddington is not clear, but nothing resulted.

Work on a Bill to Parliament for the Torrington and Okehampton Railway began in 1893 and the company was actually incorporated on 6th July 1895. The proposed line was to run from Torrington, over the track of the Marland line, through Hatherleigh and join up with the LSWR line at Fatherford, east of Okehampton. The LSWR had agreed to work the line, but after some initial work was carried out, financial troubles set in and in spite of restructuring the company, the LSWR decided that the line would not generate sufficient revenue and eventually managed to obtain an Act of Abandonment in 1907. The Holsworthy line was eventually extended on to Bude in 1898.

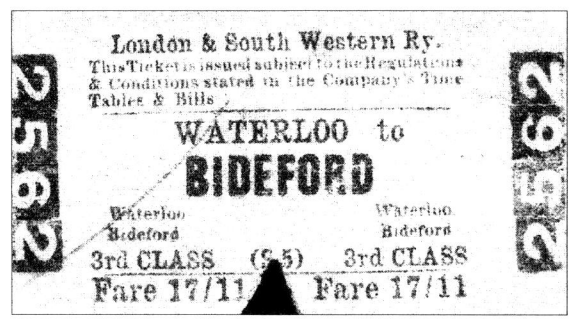

(Ian Pringle)

THE BIDEFORD, WESTWARD HO! & APPLEDORE RAILWAY

The paddle steamer "Privateer" alongside in about 1897. She ran pleasure trips out to Bideford bar and along the coast during the summer months. (Bideford Library)

Chapter 2

Plans Are Laid

Preliminary Steps

A *Gazette* article on 1st October 1895 began "Railway schemes have lost the charm of novelty in North Devon". It continued "and therefore very little has been made of the proposal to construct a steam tramway from Bideford to Westward Ho!" The article suggests that the fiasco of the events of 1870 were to blame for the apparent scepticism with which the new proposals had been received. It suggests that if the rumours were to be true that: "the gentlemen supporting the venture are Mr George Taylor of Abbotsham Court and Captain Molesworth R.N., the scheme will probably be prosecuted with vigour. Mr Taylor is the son of a noted railway contractor, and Captain Molesworth has for years been active in enterprises of this sort." (Author's note: George James Taylor, in some documents referred to as George John Taylor, was indeed the son of James Taylor, who did much work for the LSWR including the Yeovil to Exeter line, the Chard branch, the Torrington Extension Railway, and the Barnstaple to Ilfracombe line.) The article stated that surveys were under way and concludes, "The traffic between Bideford and Westward Ho! has attained proportions which promise well for the pecuniary success of a line of this character."

By the 19th November, the *Gazette* was able to report that: "preliminary steps are now being taken to obtain an Act in the next Session of Parliament conferring the necessary powers upon the promoters. The line will be a three feet gauge light railway." A description of the route then follows:

"The plans show a terminus upon Bideford Quay, a trifle the bridge side of High Street. Then the line proceeds down the Quay, starting across from the Bandstand to Northam Causeway near the foot of Raleigh Hill. Proceeding up Kenwith Valley the line will work round by Abbotsham Cliffs into Westward Ho! Thence the rails will be laid so as to serve the Golf Pavilion, and further on will draw in by the foot of Bone Hill, and then by way of the Gas Works and the R.N.R. Battery will enter Appledore finding a terminus not far from the National Schools, practically right in the centre

The Quay in about 1892/3. The young saplings were planted in 1891. (Bideford Library)

of the village. It should be noted also that it is proposed to run a set of rails along Bideford Quay inside the Promenade for goods traffic, the idea being that ships shall unload merchandise for Westward Ho! and places en route, direct into the trucks at the Quayside."

A comment is made regarding the effect the new line would have on Messrs. Dymond, Son & Blackmore's buses. The article continues by explaining that the somewhat devious route to Appledore via Westward Ho! was decided upon to avoid costly tunnelling through solid rock which a more direct route would necessitate. The engineer was reported to be Mr Jervis M.I.C.E., who had estimated the overall cost of the project, including rolling stock and equipment, at about £15,000.

James Thomas Jervis was 50 years of age at this time and a civil engineer of very wide experience. He started his working life as a pupil of P.J. Margary – one of Isambard Kingdom Brunel's engineers – on the South Devon Railway. His subsequent career saw him working in the Indus Valley in India, in South Wales, Hungary, Rumania, Moldavia, Argentina, Italy, Sweden and Norway. He was also heavily involved in the construction of the Midland & Great Northern line in Norfolk. As well as railways, his works included gas works, quays, landing stages and hydraulic machinery. He was elected a member of the Institution of Civil Engineers on 5th December 1893.

At this point it is worth quoting from the Notice advising of application to Parliament for the new Bill. This formed part of the *Book of Reference* which listed all the parcels of land that would be required for the construction of the railway. After the description of the route the Notice continued:

"To empower the Company to work said intended Railway or Tramway No. 1 by animal power, and by electricity, steam, pneumatic, gas, oil, or any mechanical power, and partly by one such power, and partly by another such power. In the case of electricity, such power is intended to be applied by means of the rails of the said railway or tramway and of conductors placed under, on, or above the surface of the streets, in connection with a generating station or generating stations, or to be carried with the carriages; <u>in the case of steam</u>, such power is intended to be carried with the carriages or applied <u>by means of locomotives</u> or of cables, wires, or ropes placed under the surface of the streets and in connection with a stationary engine or stationary engines; and in the case of pneumatic, gas or oil, or other mechanical power, the power is intended to be carried with the carriages or applied by means of locomotives." (Author's underlining.)

A view of the Quay from East-the-Water taken around 1896, after the building of the Art School. Note the large number of boats moored up. (Bideford Library)

PLANS ARE LAID

The option to use steam power is unequivocally stated.

Just before the Christmas of 1895, the new railway company's solicitors wrote to the Bideford Town Council outlining the benefits of the new railway and seeking to gain the Council's support for their Bill. The advantages to the town and surrounding area were put forward and mention was made of the lack of noise from the engines. Speed limits of eight miles per hour on the Quay, but "from the new Technical School speed may be increased to 25 miles per hour". The Council formally "dissented" so as to allow it the right to appear before Parliament to argue any matters of dissent. Later in the article the *Gazette* confides in its readers:

"We are betraying no confidence in saying that the ultimate aim of the promoters of this Bideford, Westward Ho! and Appledore line is a direct connection with the London and South-Western Railway Station across the water. This will involve a new bridge, and what more natural than that the Bridge Trustees, or the County Council, should build one jointly?"

The article questions whether the existing road bridge should be torn down and a new road/rail bridge built or a new bridge built for the railway. It suggests that the new line could end in a siding at the station to enable easy transfer of passengers as occurred with the Lynton & Barnstaple line. All this presumably still assumes that the line is to be of 3ft gauge and that the "direct connection" mentioned earlier would not be as envisaged in 1870 when Captain Molesworth put forward his plans for a swing bridge.

One can understand this whole matter became rather a contentious point in the town and on 14th January 1896, the Town Council considered a report from the committee appointed to consider the matter of the new railway. The report recommended acceptance of the scheme provided "that the promoters fill in the Pill (the Kenwith stream which ran into the river at the end of the Quay) place their lines along the centre of the filled portion, and run their train over it as a tramway". This condition apparently took the promoters by surprise for although the matter had been discussed before, Mr Taylor – for the promoters – stated that they could not fill the Pill and lay the railway over it. Captain Molesworth thought it too much to ask that they should be asked to carry out: "a public improvement. He was reminded that if Bideford had not laid out a considerable sum to widen the Quay, the Railway could not have run over it."

A compromise was eventually reached whereby the Railway Company was to use the excavations for the cutting near Abbotsham Cliffs to partly fill the Pill and the Council would make up the rest. This suggestion was subsequently agreed upon with the Council thus allowing a Bill to proceed. By early February the *Gazette* reported that the engineer Mr. J.T. Jervis C.E. had calculated the total cost of the venture at £14,957. The line to be single throughout, of 3ft gauge and as far as practicable worked as a light railway. A capital of £50,000 was to be raised which would include the cost of erecting "hotels in Appledore, Westward Ho! and Abbotsham and in providing omnibuses and vehicles". Five years were allowed for construction and borrowing was to be limited to £16,666. Interest on the shares was to be paid out of capital "at a rate not exceeding £750 in every £12,500 of capital raised".

One of the objections initially raised to the Railway was that of the level crossing at Northam Causeway, near Raleigh Gate. At a meeting of the Northam Urban District Council on Saturday 1st February 1896, Mr. Jervis, the Company's engineer, and Mr Lawman, the Company's appropriately named solicitor, were interviewed as to the eight planned level crossings. In a lengthy article, the *Gazette* reported on the meeting in its issue the following Tuesday. Strong feelings were expressed against level crossings on the grounds that they presented a danger to the public, and it was suggested that the line should be made to cross the road by means of a bridge.

Mr Jervis pointed out that this would increase the costs of the line considerably, quoting a figure of £2,000 as the extra for providing a bridge. Eventually the meeting passed a resolution on the matter:

"That this Council offers no opposition to the proposed Bill, provided every safe guard is used to prevent unnecessary delay to carriages and passengers on the roads in the district, and that it be an instruction to the promoters to consider the desirability to construct the proposed line nearer Northam Village."

Two weeks later, on 18th February 1896, the *Gazette* quotes an article from the *Western Morning News* on the subject of the railway. Headed "WESTWARD HO! RAILWAY AND HARBOUR" the article sets out details of the scheme as provided to it by George Taylor the promoter, so as to assist:

"those who may have been misled by statements which have appeared. As we have already announced, the line – a bonâ fide light railway of 3ft. gauge – will start at about at the middle of Bideford Quay, will cross the marshes and Northam Causeway, and up through Kenwith Valley, by Abbotsham Court, through a deep cutting to Cornborough and into Westward Ho! on the Clovelly side. So far from the railway taking five years to construct, as has been stated, Mr Taylor says it will be made in twelve months from the Act being obtained. Five years is the time which the Act will cover without renewal."

Quashing rumours that the railway will not be made, the

THE BIDEFORD, WESTWARD HO! & APPLEDORE RAILWAY

article quotes Mr Taylor as saying that an £800 deposit has been lodged with the authorities and the Act itself will cost another £1,000. Would the promoters expend this amount "if they did not mean business?"

It is quite clear that they did mean business, for the Bideford, Westward Ho! & Appledore Railway Bill had been presented to Parliament on the previous day – 17th February 1896. Other comments regarding the route are made, but the article then continues to discuss the planned harbour works at Westward Ho! The site was given as to the west of the Nassau Baths, on the Abbotsham side of Westward Ho! and the harbour was to enclose about 1½ acres of water. Clearly major works were planned here for:

"the proposed structure will be of masonry, bedded in the rock, and is estimated to cost from £15,000 to £20,000. A breakwater bending slightly towards Appledore will be 300 feet long, with a varying thickness of 34 feet at the base to 16 feet at the top, rising by a curve sufficient to break the force of the water. A parapet will be 4 feet high and 2 feet 6 inches in depth."

The breakwater was to be built into the rock to a depth of 14ft and be 8ft above high water. At half-tide there would be 15ft of water "sufficient to land passengers". A jetty – 200ft long – was to be provided on the Westward Ho! side. It was calculated that about 20,000 yards of rock would have to be excavated for the harbour and twenty to thirty ton concrete blocks would be used in the construction of the breakwater. It was planned to construct the blocks on site. 15,000 yards of masonry would be needed for the structure and some 10,000 yards of infill needed between the Quay and the main road, which would be taken from the harbour excavations.

An Act of Parliament was not required for the building of the harbour, and the Board of Trade had apparently sanctioned the construction, provided it did not interfere with the navigation of Bideford bar. The finished harbour was seen as an added attraction for the resort, and it was hoped that "many yachts may be expected to take advantage of its shelter". The article concludes that house and hotel building work was apparent at Westward Ho! and that a railway and harbour would greatly stimulate such development.

The Bill for the railway came before the Examiner in the House of Commons the previous week, and passed Standing Orders. In early March that year – 1896 – the House of Commons Select Committee on Unopposed Bills considered the Bill, and the *Gazette* printed a report on the proceeding on 10th March. The various clauses of the Bill were each considered. Capital of £50,000 in 5,000 shares of £10 each was sought, and borrowing powers up to £16,666 limited to 33⅓% of the issued capital. Passenger fares would be 3d per mile (first class), 2d per mile (second class) and 1d per mile (third class).

"For the conveyance of merchandise the maximum rates are:– For 7lb., 3d.; 14lb., 5d.; 28lb., 7d.; 56lb., 9d.; and above that weight up to 500 lb. the company may demand any sum they think fit."

Powers were also sought to provide hotel accommodation at Abbotsham, Westward Ho! and Appledore and refreshment-rooms at the stations, subject to approval by 75% of the shareholders. Interest on capital was to be paid during the construction period, but not exceeding £750 in respect of each portion of £12,500 of capital raised. This is as noted earlier and works out at 6%. This point was the subject of some discussion and was later amended to 3%. Counsel for the Speaker queried the overall cost per mile, which he thought excessive at £7,200. It was pointed out that the overall costs included the provision of hotels, etc. The resulting harbour would have been quite impressive and no doubt attracted a good water-borne clientele. Unfortunately the harbour scheme came to naught, but it is interesting to conjecture as to how Westward Ho! might have continued to flourish if such a scheme had gone ahead.

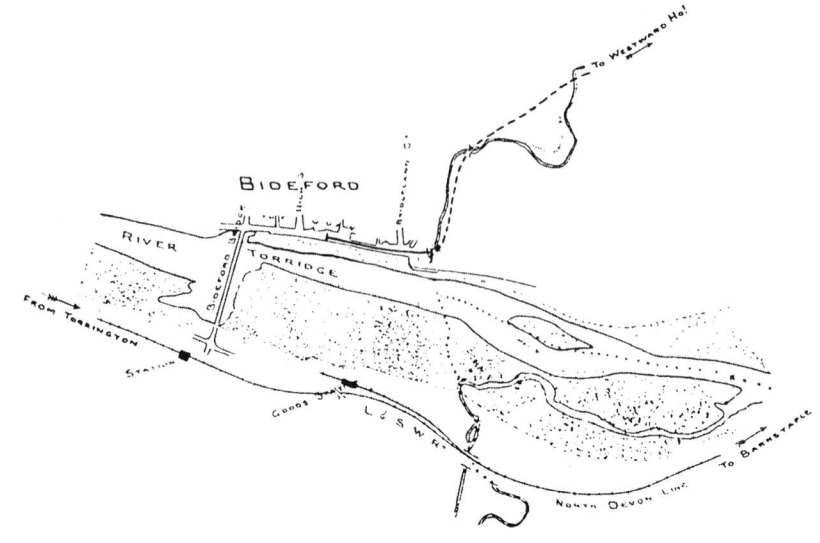

The official B.E.T. map of Bideford showing the LSWR and the new railway.

PLANS ARE LAID

The Act is Passed

After some work in the committee stages, a few minor amendments were made to the Bill, and on 21st May 1896 it received the Royal Assent as the Bideford, Westward Ho! & Appledore Railway Act, 1896 and the railway officially came into existence. In view of the importance of the Act as it affected the actual construction and operation of the railway and particularly as its various clauses affected relations with the local council virtually throughout the life of the line, it is worth considering the main clauses of the Act in a little detail at this stage. The Preamble to the Act of Parliament reads:

"Whereas the construction of the railway or tramway and railways herein-after described in the County of Devon would be of public and local advantage:

"And whereas the several persons hereinafter named with others are willing at their own expense to carry the undertaking by this Act authorised into execution on being incorporated into a Company for the purpose:

"And whereas it is expedient that the powers in this Act contained relative to the providing by the Company of hotels and hotel accommodation and refreshment rooms and omnibuses and vehicles and the granting and holding of licences should be conferred upon the Company:

"And whereas it is expedient that the Company should be authorised subject to the provisions of this Act to pay interest on the amount paid up from time to time in respect of the shares in their capital as by this Act provided:

"And whereas plans and sections showing the lines and levels of the railway or tramway and railways authorised by this Act and also a book of reference to the plans containing the names of the owners and lessees or reputed owners and lessees and of the occupiers of the lands required or which may be taken for the purposes or under the powers of this Act were duly deposited with the clerk of the peace for the county of Devon and are herein-after respectively referred to as the deposited plans and sections and book of reference…."

Section 4 of the Act names George Mill Frederick Molesworth, George James Taylor and Charles Eagle Bott "and all other persons or corporations who have already subscribed to or shall hereafter become proprietors in the undertaking" as being united into "The Bideford, Westward Ho! and Appledore Railway Company".

(Author's note: Acts of Parliament often omit commas, and, in the original, this Act does not show one after the name Molesworth. This has lead in the past to the incorrect assumption that George Mill and Frederick Molesworth were 2 separate people.)

Section 5 reads:

"Subject to the provisions of this Act the Company may make and maintain the line and according to the levels shown on the deposited plans and sections herein-after described with all proper stations sidings approaches works and conveniences connected therewith and may enter upon take and use such of the lands delineated on the said plans and described in the deposited book of reference as may be required for that purpose.

Digging up the roadway on the Quay preparatory to laying the rails. (Rob Dark Collection)

THE BIDEFORD, WESTWARD HO! & APPLEDORE RAILWAY

Spectators watch as work progresses! (Rob Dark Collection)

"The Railway herein-before referred to and authorised by this Act is –

"Railway or Tramway (No. 1) one furlong nine chains and fifty links in length of which three chains is double line and one furlong six chains and fifty links is single line commencing in the parish and borough of Bideford in the centre of the street running alongside and parallel with the quay at Bideford aforesaid at a point twelve yards or thereabouts measured in a northerly direction from an imaginary line extended from the westernmost end of the bridge known as Bideford Bridge and in a line with the northern parapet of that bridge to the centre of the roadway of such street and terminating in the said parish and borough of Bideford at a point five yards or thereabouts measured in an easterly direction from the north-east corner and in line with the north face of the building known as the municipal technical school in Bideford;

"Railway (No. 2) four miles three furlongs nine chains and ninety links in length commencing at the point of termination of the said Railway or Tramway No. 1 and terminating in the parish of Northam at a point seventy-nine yards or thereabouts measured in a northerly direction along the west side of the roadway leading from Nelson Terrace to the Pebbleridge at Westward Ho! in the said parish of Northam from an imaginary line drawn from the north-west corner and in line with the north front of the said Nelson Terrace;

"Railway (No. 3) two miles three furlongs and 4.20 chains in length commencing at the point of termination of Railway No. 2 and terminating in the said parish of Northam at a point twenty yards or thereabouts from the north-west corner of the national school in Appledore measured in a westerly direction in line with the north face of the said schoolhouse.

"6. Subject to the provisions of this Act contained as to the Railway or Tramway No. 1 by this Act authorised and to the provisions of Sections 28 and 29 of the Regulation of Railways Act 1868 the Railway may if so resolved by the Directors of the Company be constructed and worked as a light Railway.

"7. The Railway shall be made and maintained on a gauge of three feet. Provided that it shall be lawful for the Company at any time hereafter with the previous approval of the Board of Trade to increase the gauge from three feet to any gauge not exceeding four feet eight and a half inches. Provided further that so much of Section thirty-four of the Tramways Act 1870 as limits the extent of the carriage used on any tramway beyond the outer edge of the wheels of such carriage shall not apply to carriages used on the Railway."

There then follow the sections relating to share capital, shares and matters relating thereto, and regulations as to directors and meetings.

PLANS ARE LAID

Laying the track for the siding point towards the Pill end of the Quay. Note that the rails are laid on longitudinal sleepers. (Chris Leigh Collection)

Section 31 limits the period allowed for compulsory purchase of land to three years from the date of the Act.

Sections 32 and 33 specify the points at which level crossing of roads is permitted and also specify the maximum permitted gradients allowed where certain roads needed to be brought up to the level of the railway for the purposes of making a level crossing of those roads.

Clause 38 is the longest in the entire Act and relates solely to the railway or tramway No. 1, that is, the section on the Quay. It covers a great number of matters, many of which were to prove contentious. Section A of this clause *allows* the use of animal power for moving carriages but also, *with Board of Trade approval* (Author's italics), the use of steam, electric or other mechanical power. Penalties are laid down for the use of steam power without prior approval.

Section C provides for the Board of Trade to make or amend byelaws in respect of:
- The use of a bell, whistle or other warning apparatus
- Bringing trains to a stand at intersections and/or where horses may become frightened, or impending danger
- Regulating "entry to and exit from, and accommodation in the carriages", and the "protection of passengers from any machinery or motor used for drawing or propelling such carriages"
- Provision for the proper publicity and display of such byelaws.

Section E allows the Board of Trade to alter speed limits from those laid down in the Tramways Act, 1870.

Section G stipulates that the Company shall "give 2 months notice" to the road authority of any intention to use "any power other than animal power". Note there is no requirement to seek approval from the road authority or from any authority other than the Board of Trade as laid down in Section A.

Requirements are laid down as to agreements with the road authority for maintenance of the roadway and that the tops of the rails must be level with the roadway. Section J makes provision for Board of Trade inspection and approval before the tramway can be opened for public traffic.

The Company is also required to give notice to the road authority of its intention to open or break up any roadway for the purpose of laying rails, and detailed plans are to be provided to the road authority and the Board of Trade of the work to be carried out.

Provision to make additional crossing places is provided in Section Q, with restrictions given as to clearances between the track and footpaths.

The finishing touches are added to the area around the point. (Chris Leigh Collection)

Interestingly, Section 39 contains detailed provisions for the use of electric power if required, presumably if the Company had desired of converting to an overhead electric tramway system.

The Corporation of Bideford was given specific protection under Section 41 of the Act as follows:

"(1) The Company shall not without the consent of the corporation in writing under their seal construct that portion of Railway or Tramway No. 1 which lies between its point of commencement and a point on the Broad Quay opposite the south corner of Mr. Trewin's stores on the Broad Quay.

"(2) The Company shall not use the said Railway or Tramway for goods traffic but may for the purposes of such traffic make and use a siding from the said Railway or Tramway No. 1 at or near its termination to a point on the portion of the quay outside the iron railing lying between the promenade and the river opposite the north corner of Mrs. Freeman's house as shown by a red line on the plan signed by James William Lowther Esquire the Chairman of the Committee of the House of Commons to whom the Bill for this Act was referred and which plan has been deposited in the Private Bill Office and such siding shall be laid and maintained in such manner that the uppermost surface of the rail shall be on a level with the surface of the road:

"(3) Railway No. 2 by this Act authorised shall for a distance of 200 yards from its commencement be constructed as a tramway and shall be laid near the centre of the new roadway intended to be constructed by the corporation on the site of the River Pill as the requirements of the Board of Trade will admit of and the Company shall to the extent to which it is intended to construct such last-mentioned portion of Railway No. 2 on the said new roadway and within three years from the passing of this Act fill in at their own expense so much of the River Pill as shall be required for the purpose of the construction of so much of the said Railway No. 2 as shall be laid upon the said intended new road and shall in all things complete such filling in to the reasonable satisfaction of the corporation or their surveyor for the time being so as to admit so much of the said Railway No. 2 being laid on the said new road and the provisions of the Tramways Act 1870 incorporated with this Act and of Section 38 of this Act shall apply to so much of Railway No. 2 as shall be constructed as a tramway."

A five-year construction period was allowed in Section 42.

"(4) The Corporation shall so far as they legally can give all such licenses and consents as may be necessary to enable the Company expeditiously to carry out the filling in of so much of the River Pill and the completion thereof so that such

PLANS ARE LAID

Laying the line from the Quay round on to the Pill. The Art School is on the left with the bandstand in the background. The method of laying the rail is clearly seen in this photograph. The longitudinal sleepers were tied together at intervals. (Chris Leigh Collection)

filling in and completion shall cause no delay to the construction and opening of the said railway:

"(5) The Railway Clauses Consolidation Act 1845, and Part I (construction of a railway) of the Railway Clauses Act 1863 incorporated within this Act shall not apply to Railway or Tramway No. 1 or so much of Railway No. 2 as shall be constructed as a tramway under the provisions of this section and the Company shall not acquire any right other than that of user of or over any street or road along or across which Railway or Tramway No. 1 and so much of Railway No. 2 as aforesaid shall be laid."

Section 44 confirms rates for carriage of merchandise to be as those allowed under the London and South Western Railway Company (Rates and Charges) Order 1891.

Section 46 sets out the rates to be charged for small parcels (other than those of perishable merchandise exceeding fifty-six pounds weight which is covered by the LSWR Order):
- For any parcel not exceeding seven pounds in weight – threepence
- Over seven, but not exceeding fourteen pounds – fivepence
- Over fourteen, but not exceeding twenty-eight pounds – sevenpence
- Over twenty-eight, but not exceeding fifty-six pounds – ninepence
- Over fifty-six pounds, but not exceeding five hundred pounds, the Company was allowed to "demand any sum they think fit".

Passenger fares were covered in Section 46:
- First class passengers – threepence per mile
- Second class passengers – twopence per mile
- Third class passengers – one penny per mile

"For every passenger carried on the railway for a less distance than four miles the Company may charge as for four miles and for every fraction of a mile beyond four miles or any greater number of miles shall be deemed a mile."

A baggage allowance of one hundred and twenty pounds for first class passengers, one hundred pounds for second class and sixty pounds for third class was made.

THE BIDEFORD, WESTWARD HO! & APPLEDORE RAILWAY

The powers of the Company were extended by Section 49 to "acquire take on lease erect provide hold enjoy and maintain an hotel or hotels at Abbotsham Westward Ho! and Appledore or any of those places as part of their undertaking and may provide refreshment rooms at their stations".

Licences for the sale of wines, spirits, etc were to be granted to the Company's nominees for the sale of wines, spirits, etc at the hotels and refreshment rooms. Section 51 authorised the Company to "purchase and acquire work and use horses and omnibuses and other vehicles".

Section 52 allows for the payment of interest to shareholders on the amount of paid up shares (up to a maximum of three per cent) out of capital during the period of construction.

Finally, "The SCHEDULE referred to in the foregoing Act.

"Every engine used on the tramway shall be fitted with such mechanical appliances for preventing the motive power of such engine from operating and from bringing such engine and any carriage drawn or propelled by such engine to a stand as the Board of Trade may from time to time think sufficient.

"Every engine used on the tramway shall have its number shown in some conspicuous part thereof and shall be fitted –
- With an indicator by means of which the speed shall be shown;
- With a suitable fender to push aside obstructions;
- With a special bell whistle or apparatus to be sounded as a warning when necessary; and
- With a seat for the driver of such engine so placed in front of such engine as to command the fullest possible view of the road before him.

"Every such engine shall be free from noise produced by blast or clatter of machinery and the machinery shall be concealed from view at all points above four inches from the level of the rails and all fire used on such engine shall be concealed from view.

"Every carriage used on the tramway shall be so constructed as to provide for the safety of passengers and for their safe entrance to exit from and accommodation in such carriage and their protection from the machinery of any engine used for drawing or propelling such carriage.

"The Board of Trade shall on the application of the local authority and may on complaint made by any person from time to time inspect any engine or carriage used on the tramway and the machinery therein and may whenever they think fit prohibit the use on the tramway of any such engine or carriage which in their opinion may not be safe for use on the tramway.

"The speed at which engines and carriages may be driven or propelled along the tramway shall not exceed the rate of eight miles an hour.

"The speed at which engines and carriages may pass through moveable facing points on the tramway shall not exceed four miles an hour."

We have already heard that James Thomas Jervis M.I.C.E. had been appointed as Engineer to the Company and it appears that Charles Chadwell of Richmond Chambers, Blackburn in Lancashire was appointed contractor. His resident engineer was to be A.S. Chapman. Surveyors were soon in evidence in the area, although little actual construction work could be started for some time. The promoters were also working upon their plans for an additional line to Clovelly for which they were preparing a new Bill to go before Parliament. They envisaged work on both lines being undertaken simultaneously as the two lines were to be run as one. Also, not all the land had been acquired, partly due to the high prices being demanded by the owners, and it was some two years before it was all available and workmen were fully employed in railway building.

Meanwhile, a general atmosphere of mini "railway mania" seemed to be circulating in North Devon in 1897, for the *Gazette* of 30th November reported "Railway schemes are 'in the air' – of Devonshire at any rate". The article suggests this was brought about by the facility then available for the construction of "light railways" under recent legislation. There had been no official definition of a "light railway" although the objective of such was clear, to open up a rural or undeveloped area at minimal cost. Certainly lower standards of engineering would be used, and requirements as to signalling, stations, level crossings and the like would be minimal. These allowances would be balanced by restrictions as to train speeds and weight of locomotives and rolling stock. It was not until the Railway Construction Facilities Act of 1864 that such relaxation in standards of construction, etc was allowed and the first official use of the term "light railway" did not occur until the 1868 Regulation of Railways Act.

Various Light Railway and Tramways Acts came into force between 1864 and 1883, making the construction of railways in certain circumstances much easier and cheaper. There was however a national feeling that some official encouragement should be given to the promotion of light railways in order to facilitate the opening up of those areas not yet provided with railway connections and the 1896 Light Railways Act reinforced the previous legislation and made provision for the authorisation of such lines without the need for Parliamentary approval. Three Commissioners were appointed to approve new schemes.

PLANS ARE LAID

Returning to the *Gazette*, the article of 30th November 1897 continued by mentioning the three prospective lines then under consideration: the Torrington and Okehampton, the Bideford, Westward Ho! & Appledore, and the Bideford & Clovelly. This latter line – mentioned earlier – was planned as a branch off the B.W.Ho & A. Railway, although it was to be worked as the "main line" with the line to Westward Ho! and Appledore being the subsidiary route. Running powers from Bideford would take it about 1½ miles to Kenwith, where it would turn off and head towards the coast. Thence the route would be Rixlade, Gipsy Lane, Fairy Cross, Horn's Cross, and Bucks Cross to Clovelly Dykes. The total run was to be 10½ miles after the junction with the B.W.Ho & A.

The line would be 3ft gauge, "but the promoters will have the power to make it the standard 4 feet 8½ inches gauge, with the consent of the Board of Trade". This clause regarding gauge was also included in the B.W.Ho & A Railway Act, but seems to have escaped much attention, either by the Press or the local council, but this situation was soon to change.

A meeting of the Bideford Rural District Council on 15th February 1898 saw Captain Molesworth and Mr Jervis being interviewed on this proposed new Bill for the Bideford & Clovelly line. The main area of contention was that of level crossings, and after discussion, Mr Jervis agreed that bridges would be built to replace the planned crossings. No mention is made of the additional expense involved. A member of the council made the point that the railway would be much better if it connected with the LSWR main line to avoid costs of transhipment. Captain Molesworth responded that it was intended "when the line was completed, to take a bridge over the Torridge, and effect a junction with the L. and S. W. R. so that in time anyone would be able to go from London to Clovelly by train without changing". Council opposition to the Bill would be withdrawn. It would seem that the fact had still not registered that through travel over a new bridge in Bideford would mean a continuous line of standard gauge railway! By 5th April 1898, the *Gazette* was able to report that the Select Committee of the House of Lords had considered the Bideford & Clovelly Bill. Their Lordships had adjourned their deliberations, but the Act finally became law on 25th July 1898.

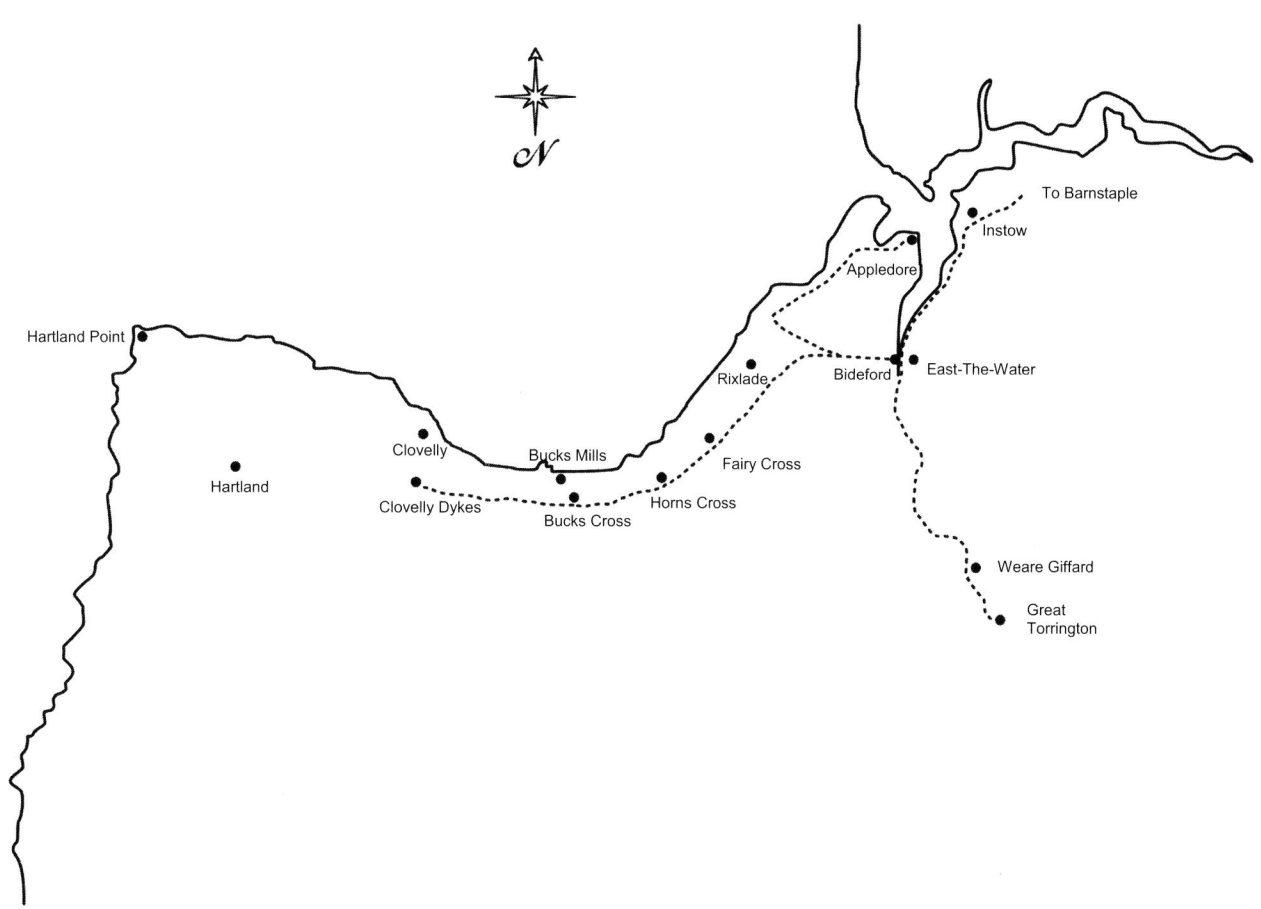

Outline map of the proposed Clovelly Branch. (Martin Dowding)

THE BIDEFORD, WESTWARD HO! & APPLEDORE RAILWAY

Construction

It is not clear when actual construction work started in earnest on the Bideford, Westward Ho! & Appledore line, but it must be assumed that this was either late in 1897 or early in 1898. It does seem however that this was commenced from both the Bideford and Westward Ho! ends of the line and at several other points, notably the section near Abbotsham where a deep cutting was required through the rock. Groundwork must have been proceeding well for a shipment of rails was unloaded on to Bideford Quay from the *S.S. Snipe* on or about 12th May 1898. Four months later *The Lannoy* of West Hartlepool discharged a load of timber sleepers at the quayside.

As a slight aside, the *S.S. Snipe*, a Glasgow registered screw driven steamer, was apparently a regular visitor to the area for she is recorded as leaving Newport in South Wales in November 1898 with a cargo of rails, tinplate, etc. bound for Birkenhead. It is not known if any of the rail was destined for Bideford, but unfortunately the *Snipe* ran aground on the Cardiff sands on 9th November and suffered extensive damage. According to *Lloyd's List* for 11th November she "got off without assistance" but the damage was severe enough for the same entry to record, "Vessel will discharge and go into dry dock." She was presumably repaired and put back into service as she appears in *Lloyd's Register* for 1900/1901.

On 17th May 1898, the *Gazette* reported the opening, on the previous Wednesday, 11th May, of the lovely Lynton and Barnstaple line, built to a gauge of 1ft 11 ½in and not the 3ft as conjectured earlier. An aside, headed "By-the-bye" at the end of the note announced that construction of the Railway was "proceeding apace" with a substantial portion of the cutting in the Abbotsham – Westward Ho! section being completed.

On Tuesday 24th January 1899, the statutory meeting of shareholders of the Bideford & Clovelly Railway Company were updated on progress to date. Working drawings and land plans had been ordered from the Engineer, Mr Jervis, but progress had been slowed "by the very inclement weather". However it was reported that the Company were entering negotiations for letting the construction contract, and discussions were being held with the owners for purchase of the necessary land.

A report in the *Gazette* for 16th May 1899 sheds a considerable amount of light on the actual construction of the new line to Westward Ho!, for it contains details of a walk along the route of the line by the *Gazette's* correspondent,

Construction work always attracts small boys! Note the rail bending jig leaning on the tool box. A group of workmen is just visible in the centre distance. (Rob Dark Collection)

PLANS ARE LAID

who was accompanied by the contractor's engineer, and contains much information and is of sufficient interest to reproduce here in full.

"A few days since the temporary rails used in constructing the Bideford and Westward Ho! railway, which were laid from the Westward Ho! and the Bideford ends, were joined, so that there is now through connection between the two places. The line is of course only temporary, and is about two feet in guage (sic), but the proper guage (sic), the laying of which will be commenced shortly, is to be 4½ feet 8 in. (sic), the sleepers 9ft, and the formation 15ft. On Saturday last, our representative walked along the line with Mr A.S. Chapman, the engineer to whom is entrusted the construction of the line. Leaving Bideford River Bank the line threads its way through the fields, and crosses Northam Causeway, near the foot of Raleigh Hill. Here a level crossing will be made with the usual gates, and a caretaker's cottage will be erected near by, so that a man may be there whenever needed. After crossing the Causeway, the line runs along with Raleigh Hill on the right hand, and North Down Hill on the left. The valley, all the way to Abbotsham Cliffs, is wooded on one hand, on the other being deep pastures. The scenery is delightful. There is another level crossing at Kenwith, similar in every respect to that on Northam Causeway. Just beyond, some heavy work has been experienced in cutting through a hill of shillett – 32ft. deep. When this piece is entirely cleared away and the banks sloped, some 8,000 tons of debris will have been removed. This debris is taken from the cutting and deposited by the help of a small engine, and a number of trucks so as to raise the formation in the valley. The mode of excavating is to first cut a portion of the bank, leaving a shelf beneath of about half the depth. Then both levels are worked together. This saves labour, and is much handier as the workmen are enabled to remove the debris easier. Near the cutting are the carpenters' and blacksmiths' sheds. The carpenters are very much in demand. More especially their work is to repair the wheel-barrows, put new handles to the picks, shovels, etc., whilst the blacksmiths have to look after the tools, i.e., keep them sharpened. For a short distance now the line goes through more open country, until when nearing the sea, there is a steep gradient of one foot in forty feet, between banks. The cutting here is some 12 to 14 feet in depth. The rocks here, as in the other cuttings, were blasted. At present a high bank partly obscures the view of the sea, but this will be removed, so that for about a mile, the passenger will be in full view of the Bristol Channel, with Lundy Island, Clovelly, and Hartland in the distance.

"The heaviest cutting on the whole line was that just outside Westward Ho! skirting the Abbotsham Cliffs. Here solid rock had to be removed, to a depth of over 20 feet, for a distance of about a quarter of a mile. On emerging from this cutting Baggy and Morte Points, and Saunton come into view. At present temporary rails stop below the Royal Hotel, but in time the line will be extended to Appledore. The distance from Bideford to Westward Ho! by this route is about 4½ miles, and that to Appledore will be about 3 miles extra. Up to the present, the line has taken about 12 months to construct, but this is in great measure owing to the fact that considerable difficulty was experienced in obtaining the necessary land, and as a matter of fact the last portion of land to complete the connection, only became the property of the Company so recently as a month ago. At numerous places, and more especially near Bideford, several culverts have had to be made so as not to interfere with the drainage of the land, and in one instance a stream had to be diverted, and a drinking trough made for cattle. All this, of course, has tended to hinder the work of construction; but now that the temporary line is laid down, and the greater portion of the formation laid, it will take but a comparatively short time to lay down the full guage (sic). Indeed this could be done in two to three months, if necessary. The rails will be fastened to the sleepers by patent 'clips'; the usual method is by 'chairs', but the clips are an improvement. The contractor for the line is Mr. Chadwell of Blackburn. There are now about 75 navvies engaged upon the work."

This fascinating description of the line and the works is invaluable to our study and provides some very useful details. The use of a temporary 2ft gauge contractor's line is not surprising but this fact has not been published before as far as can be seen. Unfortunately no further details have been able to be discovered. The amount of blasting is quite impressive and one wonders how much more work would actually have been needed if the line had been taken the shorter route directly to Appledore and then to Westward Ho! The fact that not all the land was available until practically the last minute coupled with the remarks about "very inclement weather" in the piece about the Clovelly line suggests that progress had not been too bad in the circumstances.

As work on the railway proceeded, the unrest regarding the level crossings began to surface, and on 11th July 1899 a slightly tongue-in-cheek letter appeared in the *Gazette*:

"Sir, May I draw attention to the danger of the unfenced level-crossing at the bottom of Raleigh Hill. It runs at right-angles to the road, and as it is impossible for drivers approaching Bideford from Northam, to see the line until they are practically on it, there is more than a chance that somebody will one day run into an engine puffing across the road. The engine and trucks might be hurt. I am sure the colliding vehicle would be. Yours truly, CENSOR."

Next week's paper carried a rather nicely phrased reply from Mr Chapman at the site office.

"Dear Sir, I feel that 'Censor's' letter, published in your last week's issue, calls for a reply, as it conveys the impression that the safety of the public is no (sic) secured at the level crossing.

"Permit me to say that 'Censor' is mistaken. Whenever the engine runs across the Causeway, someone is stationed on the road to stop the traffic. Moreover, the entire width of the Causeway is visible from over 50 yards up the Northam Road, which distance one would imagine would be sufficient for anyone to pull up his horse, even were he reckless enough to dash round that (or any other) corner at a high rate of speed. Yours truly, A.S. CHAPMAN."

As an aside, the issue of 25th July 1899 carried a note that: "it has been practically decided to proceed with the Clovelly Railway. There is a further scheme to extend the line to Bude. May it come quickly." The *Gazette* does seem to have been in favour of railway expansion in the area.

Battle Lines are Drawn

Construction of the railway continued through the rest of 1899 and into 1900 and by 17th April, the *Gazette* was reporting the arrival of the first locomotive to be delivered from the manufacturers. This naturally arrived on the wrong side of the river and had to be transported over the Bideford Long Bridge.

"The Bridge Feoffees, jealous for the safety of the fabric, would not consent to the engine crossing on rails, and to meet their wishes, the boiler was taken out and the engine brought across on 'road gear' in two portions. No one objects to the Feoffees insisting on every precaution essential for safety, but to a man in the street it does not appear that the passage of the engine under its own steam, on rails carefully laid in the dead centre of the bridge, would create more vibration that the passage on lumbering 'road gear', drawn by several horses."

From one of the available photographs it would seem that the carriage bodies were mounted on a primitive wooden "low-loader" and pulled through the streets and over the bridge by horses. They were then somehow manoeuvred on to their bogies which had been brought over separately and placed on the tracks.

The railway was now at an advanced stage and work was commencing on the line along the Quay, which involved digging up the roadway to lay the rails before filling in again to rail level. This seemed to be the spark to ignite the flame of opposition to the railway in the town. The *Gazette*, ever wise and considered in its reporting carried a piece in its issue of 15th May 1900 under the heading: "Notes and Notions".

"Seldom has Bideford been so perturbed as during the past week over the extension of Bideford, Westward Ho! and Appledore Line up the Quay. Only now have the burgesses appeared to realise what is involved, and the outcry is correspondingly great. The Town Council is called upon to obtain an injunction to stop the railway contractor, and to do a variety of other things, which ought to be effective if the Railway Company has no Act of Parliament to warrant them, but which, presuming that Act to be in order, and flawless, is altogether impossible. To cry over spilt milk is no remedy, and to inveigh against the Council for sins of omission and commission is equally futile, as against the Railway Company. If the Council, representing the ratepayers, consented to, or neglected to oppose, the Railway Bill in Parliament , thereby permitting the Company to secure a right to extend their line as far as Trewin's store, the Railway Company cannot now be blamed for exercising their right. It is said in some quarters that the Council consented, believing that the railway would never be made. That is ridiculous. On the other hand it is said that the Council was not properly informed of the intentions of the Company. But, having a copy of the Company's proposed Act and a plan of the route before them, the Council cannot plead ignorance. If it can be shewn that the copy of the Bill and the Plan of the route were incorrect, and differed materially from the Bill and Plan laid before Parliament, the Council may reasonably have ground for action. But is it likely that the promoters would venture to get their Act by means of a trick? The matter is one which the Council ought to enquire into very carefully, and they

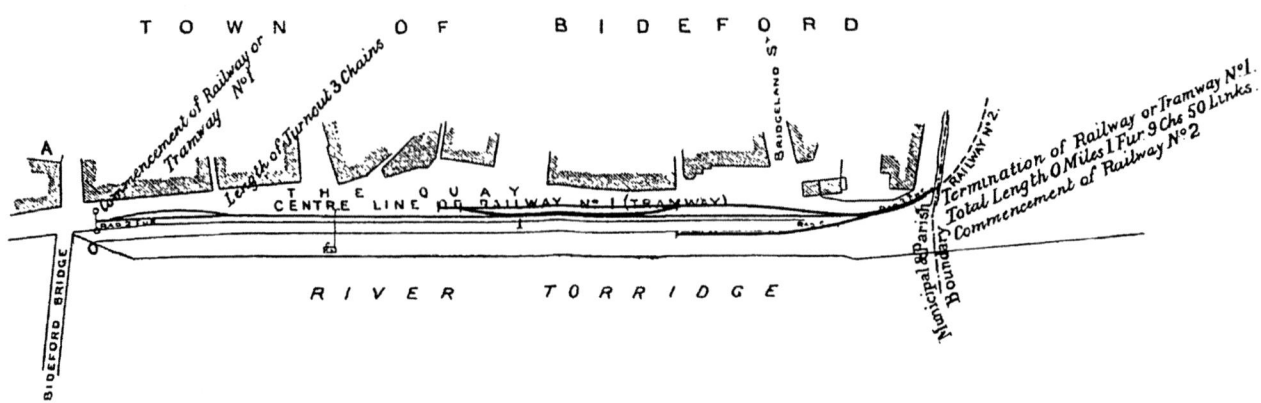

The plan of the line and loop on the Quay in its original position up to the bridge and the siding, but showing the shorter line as actually built.

PLANS ARE LAID

One of the new coaches arrives from over the bridge on its horse drawn carriage. It appears to be the flagstaff behind the coach, so it must be standing on the siding at the far end of the Quay. (Clive Fairchild Collection)

The coach is reunited with its bogies. (Chris Leigh Collection)

THE BIDEFORD, WESTWARD HO! & APPLEDORE RAILWAY

The original plan (reconstructed) of the line and loop on the Quay.

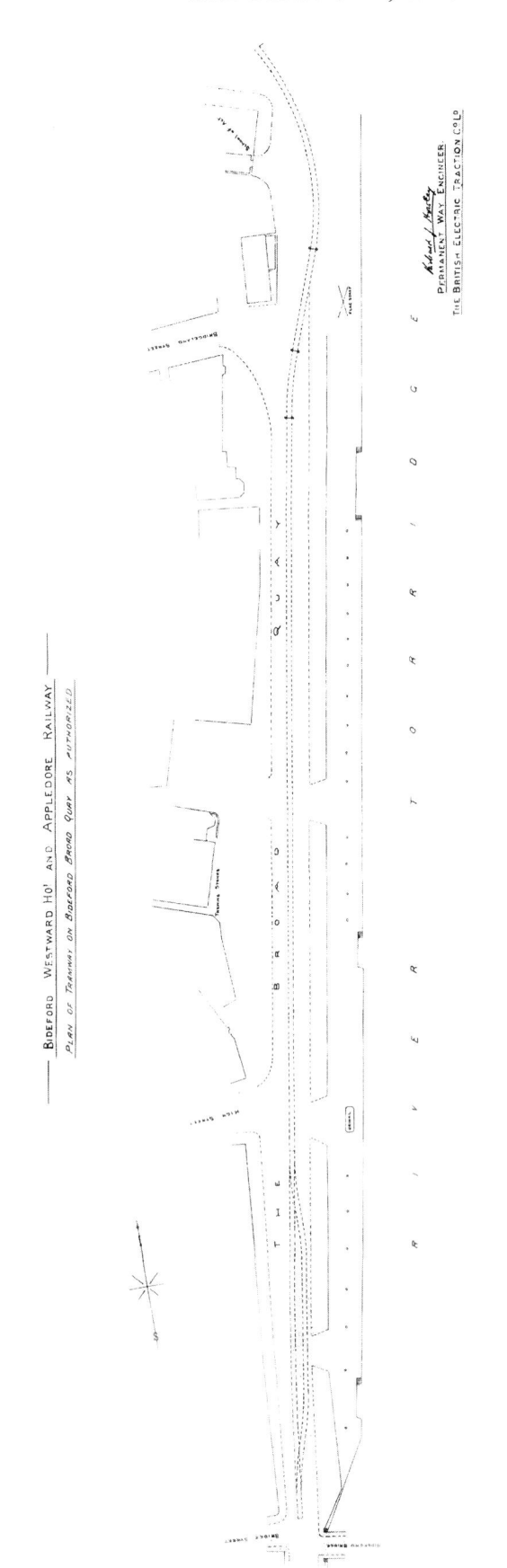

were wise in deciding, yesterday, to consider opinion of Counsel on the position, in Committee next Thursday.

"On the general question there is naturally a diversity of opinion. Not all the burgesses regard the railway as an extreme detriment. At present, appearances are all against the line, and one regrets extremely that the contractor could not have arranged to do this portion earlier, so that the ripping of the quay and consequent dishevelled condition might have been avoided now, when we are expecting visitors. Ultimately, when the road has settled again, the actual appearance of the quay will not be appreciably changed. The Company can place no structure there, and I take it the proper authorities will refuse to permit trucks, or wagons, or engines, to remain stationery there any length of time. I am aware that I have not exhausted a tithe of the objections raised. There is the question of depreciation of the value of residential property on the quay, the danger to traffic via Bridgeland Street, and the weighty objection to a steam railway in the town. But what does it avail us to howl if we cannot effect anything? The question of a loop line, however, may be a lever to achieve something.

"The naked truth of the matter, of course, is that if the Railway succeeds in its original object of developing Westward Ho! and the neighbourhood, it will be a boon to Bideford, and yield a volume of business sufficient to compensate for any reasonable grievance, whereas if the railway fails (i.e. it cannot be made to pay), it will cease running in due time, and any grievance will then be automatically removed."

This article seems to represent a measured and considered look at the situation which was about to erupt and plague the line for most of its life. There seems to have been two schools of thought in Bideford at the time: the one opposed to the railway at all costs and determined to fight it all the way, and those prepared to accept the line subject to negotiation on various matters.

The next week, the *Gazette* carried another article, setting out the position as it saw it and reporting on the Council meeting held on the previous Thursday evening. The article started by outlining the position regarding the line on the Quay. Originally the Company had wanted to run along the Quay almost to the bridge with a run-round loop to allow one engine per train working. In the face of Council opposition, they agreed to move the terminus back, roughly half way along, but the revised plan omitted to show a run-round loop. Later, the Council agreed, in return for a promise by the Company not to erect any buildings on the Pill, to a change of gauge to 4ft 8½in "in view of eventual junction with the London and South-Western Railway across the river". The article continued with reporting that Council's opinion was that, "as no 'turnout' was shown on the second plan…the Company has no right to construct one". The

PLANS ARE LAID

Company's reply was that the shortening of the line implied that the original form of terminus with a run-round loop would be restored, in order to comply with Board of Trade requirements not to propel passenger trains from behind.

It should also be remembered that there was power to lay a short siding at the northern end of the Quay and that also in dispute was whether the line should run down the centre of the Quay or towards the edge, on the promenade. The article concluded by reporting that the resident engineer, Mr Chapman was trying to complete the line by the end of the month – May, and that all three locomotives had been delivered. The locomotive and carriage sheds were being erected.

A letter from a visitor to the town in the same issue of the paper echoed the views of the opponents of the extension up the Quay. The matter of what should be laid where on the Quay was now to become the subject of intense discussion for the next few years as a study of the *Bideford Gazette* and Council Minutes will show. On 25th May 1900 the paper reported that Mr Tattersill – a local Councillor – had approached the Railway Company unofficially to see if a way could be found round the disagreements over the positioning of the rails on the Quay. The bargaining position being that if the Council agreed to let the Company to lay rails up the Quay, then they should agree not to put in a run-round loop. A meeting between the two parties was being suggested.

Under the "Notes and Notions" column in its 3rd July issue, the paper reported on the proposed meeting of ratepayers to be held on Friday, 13th July. Again the *Gazette* was considered in its report, for it commented that the proposed motion to be put before the meeting "to consider the proposed Railway on the Pill and Quay, and to pass such resolutions as may be deemed expedient" was rather too wide a brief. It reminded readers that the railway Company already had the power in the Act to run along the Quay and that to get them to change their route to run along the promenade was a matter for negotiation not dictate. Readers were reminded that when bargaining with a man, "it is not good policy to wring one's fist in his face".

The next week's issue carried a quite lengthy article in advance of the proposed meeting and continued the cautionary position of the previous article and suggested that the meeting was "mischievous" in its intent. The Council's aim of restricting the railway to the promenade side of the Quay and off the roadway would be accepted by the Company, the article suggested, if they were allowed to run as far as the bridge (no doubt as a base for bridging the river towards the LSWR station), but this was not acceptable to the Council. As far as "nearly to the bottom of High Street" would be acceptable the paper suggested. But now it seemed that the Company had applied to the Board of Trade to use steam power on the Quay. This also was not acceptable, but could be used as a bargaining tool.

The events of the meeting on Friday, 13th July were duly reported in the following week's paper. In view of the nature of the meeting, it is possible that the date was an unfortunate choice. After a preliminary jibe at the *Gazette's* comments from the previous week, Councillor Heard set out the background to the railway. The general tone of his speech was that the Railway Company was the villain of the piece riding roughshod over the people of Bideford. The first area of concern appeared to be the change of gauge, from an original reported one of 2ft 8in, to 3ft and then standard gauge. The use of the road on the Quay for the railway was objectionable and if it must be there it should run near the Quay wall at the edge of the promenade. It was felt that the line should really stop on Curtis's Marsh (The Pill), and not turn the corner on to the Quay at all. The fact that the Company had certain rights under the Act did not seem to be seen as necessarily proving an insurmountable problem to those present. The conduct of the previous Council in not objecting to the original Bill was not criticised and the meeting eventually passed the following resolution:

"That in the opinion of this meeting of ratepayers and inhabitants of the Borough of Bideford and neighbourhood, it be an expression to the Council of the said Borough from this meeting that the manner in which the projected line is being laid in the said Borough, by the Bideford, Westward Ho! and Appledore Railway Company, is dangerous to vehicular traffic, and that it be an instruction to the said Council that no further concessions whatever be made to the said Company, but further that such concessions as may have already been granted, or supposed to have been granted, be withdrawn so far as they legally can be. And that the Board of Trade be informed of this resolution, and that some of the concessions already made were without the knowledge or consent of the general body of inhabitants and that they be petitioned to cause an enquiry to be made into the facts of the case forthwith, being most urgent as affecting the welfare of the Borough and the safety of its inhabitants."

Whilst not included in the resolution, the proposed use of steam power on the Quay was seen as totally unacceptable.

A special meeting of the Council on the 23rd July accepted the resolution and agreed it be passed to the Board of Trade, with a note objecting to the use of steam power. Soon after this, negotiations were held between the Council and the Railway Company, but matters do not appear to have been resolved.

It was at around this time that control of the Railway Company passed into the hands of the British Electric Traction Company Ltd. Captain Molesworth remained on the board of the Company, but the rest of the old directors were replaced. It was reported also that on 16th July 1900, the

THE BIDEFORD, WESTWARD HO! & APPLEDORE RAILWAY

Preparatory work being carried out in readiness for laying the loop line on the Quay. (Rob Dark Collection)

contractor, Charles Chadwell ceased work in a dispute with the Company, which was to drag on through the courts for the next five years. Chadwell's contract was reportedly dated 9th February 1900, but clearly work was well under way by then and it is assumed that this later date refers to a new contract with the B.E.T. Company in place of the original with The Bideford, Westward Ho! and Appledore Railway Company. The Company alleged that Chadwell was in wilful default of his contract in that he had not completed the work, nor even completed purchase of all the land required. They terminated his contract and appointed another firm to complete the work. As well as monies for the work needed to complete the job, the claim included a sum in respect of loss of profits arising from the consequent late opening of the line, this having been delayed from 9th April 1900 to 18th May 1901. The contractor hotly disputed the Company's claims, but eventually lost his case, judgement being given for the plaintiffs in a sum of £7,500 with costs.

Previously, there has been no mention as to which contractor took over and finished the line, but recent research has established that the new contractor was the firm of Dick, Kerr & Company of Kilmarnock, better known as builders of locomotives and trams. It seems however that they were also involved in contracting work, John Kerr originally being a tramway contractor in his own right before he set up business with W.B. Dick. B.E.T. would no doubt have been well acquainted with Dick, Kerr & Company because of the common tramway interest, and such an appointment now seems quite logical.

In September 1900 the Council received a reply from the Local Government Board to its petition regarding the laying of the railway along the Pill without having paid compensation. The Board had replied that, under the Act, the Company had to fill in, at its own expense "so much of the River Pill as would be required for the construction of so much of the line as would be laid upon the new roadway proposed to be constructed by the Corporation on the site of the Pill". The Board of Trade had agreed to this and loaned a sum of £1,500 for the formation of a new street and for a pleasure ground. An additional £1,500 was later loaned to cover excess expenditure on the project. "The Board did not consider that any comment upon this statement of fact was necessary."

At a meeting on 24th September, the Council was advised that the Railway Company had proposed that if the

PLANS ARE LAID

Council withdrew its objections, they would agree to run on the promenade side of the Quay. If not, they would proceed as they were entitled to under the Act. It was pointed out by one Councillor that the Company had not asked permission to use steam power, merely advised their intentions. Another Councillor pointed out that steam traction engines were constantly running up and down the Quay without objections. During the meeting one Councillor accused another of telling the Railway Company that there would not be any objections to their plans. The latter denied this and a row broke out. After some further discussion, the Council accepted the compromise.

The *Gazette* of 20th November carried three separate notices of relevance to the railway plans for the county. The Torrington & Okehampton Railway was applying for an extension of time for compulsory purchase of lands, and other more minor amendments. The Bideford & Clovelly Railway were firstly applying for extension of time, power to raise additional capital and to make various amendments to its Act, but more importantly, its second notice was to announce the presentation of a Bill of Abandonment. It seems that lack of capital was to blame for the failure of the Bideford & Clovelly venture and the Bill received the necessary consent. The Directors' efforts could now be fully employed on completing the line to Westward Ho!

The ongoing questions regarding the Bideford, Westward Ho! and Appledore Railway do not really seem to have been settled to a satisfactory conclusion at all, for at the Council meeting of 26th November, the matter of the steam locomotives consuming their own smoke was raised, and after some skirmishing among those present the meeting broke up on apparent disorder. On 14th December the Council were again discussing the actual placement of the tracks on the Quay, the use of steam power and the use of existing rolling stock in what appears to have been a similarly fraught re-run of the previous meeting. This meeting seems to have been bent on inserting into any new agreement with the Railway Company, the whole of the provisions of the Tramways Act of 1870, rather than the few clauses of that Act actually included in the Bideford, Westward Ho! & Appledore Act.

It is worth noting at this stage a very strong impression gained from all these reports that Bideford Council did not really want this railway, and would oppose it at every opportunity. Whether this was because the Council felt it had been hoodwinked by the Company or, more likely, felt that it had failed to realise exactly what powers the Company had obtained under the Act and had not acted early enough to have these powers changed or removed. Either way, relations were not going to improve, and the work of construction was drawing to a close with most of the line completed, apart from the contentious section from the Pill on to the Quay.

During the first week of January 1901, the *Gazette* reported that the new railway from Bideford to Westward Ho! would be opened in time for Easter. The delay, as noted earlier was partly due to the problems with the contractor, and also "the protracted negociations (sic) with the Town Council of Bideford". On Wednesday, 2nd January however:

"a construction train was run to Westward Ho! and the superintendent of the line took the opportunity to attach a carriage, and to invite a few friends to accompany him. The run was much enjoyed. Fortunately the afternoon was fine, and a splendid view of the country and the sea was obtained. Returning between 4 and 5 o'clock, the lights at Hartland and Lundy were plainly seen. The carriages are built corridor style, the passage being in the centre and the seats are very comfortable, upholstered in the same manner as those of the Twopenny Tube."

(The "Twopenny Tube" was the nickname popularly given to the underground Central London Railway which opened in 1900. It ran some 5¾ miles from Shepherd's Bush to Bank and the nickname derived from the original fare which was a flat 2d.)

Sniping resumed almost at once after the New Year had been celebrated, with the railway company sending the Council an ultimatum regarding the railway on the Quay. This stated that unless the Council accepted the terms of an agreement drafted in October by the end of January, the Company would "at once proceed with the construction of the line on the Broad Quay as authorised by their Act". A special meeting of the Council was called for Saturday, 19th January to consider their response.

The *Gazette* of the following Tuesday reported at length the proceedings of this meeting, which initially began by discussing whether or not the Company should be allowed the use of steam power on the Quay, and if so that they should be made to lay the line along the promenade, away from the main roadway. The Company appeared to have a friend in Alderman Braund who pointed out that the Act gave the Company power to lay their line down the middle of the roadway on the quay so that the terminus was in the town. He went on:

"I don't think we should be continually putting difficulties in their way, as has been the case during the past three or four months. Personally, I feel that the railway would be a great convenience during the summer months, especially for young men who wish to go to Westward Ho! to have a dip of a morning."

On the subject of steam power it was reported that Captain Molesworth had verbally stated that the Company would use the best scientific appliances on the engines so that they consumed their own smoke. This was questioned. The

THE BIDEFORD, WESTWARD HO! & APPLEDORE RAILWAY

One of the Company's wagons is being loaded with spoil, while two more of the fleet stand further along the track. The Jarrah wood blocks used between and alongside the rails lie to the left of the picture. (Chris Leigh Collection)

facts were that the Company had the power to run down the centre of the quay but not to use steam power. This was eventually agreed. It being a Saturday morning, the worthy councillors postponed any further business until the following Thursday.

After an entreaty by the Mayor that they should try to deal with the matter once and for all, Alderman Braund proposed "that all the resolutions adopted by the Council since August 13th last, with reference to the proposed agreements with the Railway Company be rescinded". The motion was carried by a large majority with only two councillors voting against. A further resolution calling for the line to be laid on the wharf side of the quay (the promenade) with the Company's rights restricted to "user" of the quay, and that the question of steam power be left to the Board of Trade was carried. The draft agreement was then amended as per this resolution.

In March 1901, the Bideford & Clovelly Railway Bill failed to pass Standing Orders as the promoters had not been able to raise the necessary capital, nor had they exercised their powers for the compulsory purchase of land.

Back on the subject of the Westward Ho! line however, the *Gazette* reported on 12th March that the only remaining issue outstanding was that of getting the Company to accept responsibility for the upkeep of the Quay wall. The Company however, seemed to be taking the line that if the Council were forcing them to run along by the Quay wall, they should not have to be responsible for the maintenance of the wall. However, at its meeting the previous Thursday, the Council was again preoccupied with railway matters, discussing a revised agreement submitted by the Railway Company regarding the proposed transfer of the line from the broad quay to the wharf side the promenade. There were 11 clauses in the agreement, and consideration of these will reveal the then current state of thinking within the Council.

Clause 1: The Company would construct the line according to a plan submitted with the agreement, and the Council would assist the Company in obtaining Parliamentary approval. The Council agreed, but subject to their plan submitted the previous September being used. It is not certain how this differed, but presumably there were some differences.

Clause 2: The Company not to acquire any other rights other than as user of the quay. Council agreed, but with the addition that the Company should not acquire any further

PLANS ARE LAID

rights than it would have had if the railway were constructed on the quay.

Clause 3: The Company would remove the rails already laid on the quay and make good at its own expense. Agreed!

Clause 4: Completion to be as soon as possible and also that all questions of rolling stock and use of steam power be left to the Board of Trade. Agreed with the addition that Parliamentary approval for the deviation be sought to allow completion within reasonable time.

Clause 5: Construction to be carried out in such a way and precautions to be taken as to prevent damage to the sea wall, and to carry out all reasonable requirements of the Town Council for such precautions. The clause then continued "having constructed the line the Company not to be held liable for damage to the wall". Council objected to this and substituted "in the event of the sea wall being damaged by the construction or use of the railway, the Company will make good any damage".

Clause 6: The Corporation to withdraw all memorials or complaints addressed to the Board of Trade. Agreed.

Clause 7: The Corporation to agree to the Company's powers under the 1896 Act being revived and a suitable passing place be authorised at the commencement of Railway No.1 so as to provide for engines to run round the carriages: the Company to abandon this clause on obtaining power for the deviation. The Council struck out this entire clause.

Clause 8: The line to be laid with Vignole's rails and sleepers, the uppermost surface to be level with the present surface of the quay, and no setts for paving to be required. This was agreed.

Clause 9: The railway to be constructed so as to allow access for vehicular traffic to pass from the broad quay to the quayside. This was agreed.

Clause 10: The provisions of the 1896 Act to apply to such deviation as if such deviation had formed part of such Act, but any reference to Tramways Acts to be deleted. The Council struck out this clause completely.

Clause 11: The Company was to pay for all costs incurred from February 25th 1901. The Council added that all costs already incurred by its Parliamentary Agents should also be paid by the Company.

Needless to say, this did not go down well with the Railway company and they sent formal notice to the Council that they intended "breaking open the road on the Broad Quay, in order to construct the tramway" in accordance with the provisions of their Act of Parliament. The Company also advised the Council that it could not agree to the plan relating to clause 1 of the agreement and were insisting on their September plan which showed the line on the wharf side of the quay, 50ft from the bottom of High Street, but the loop line further down towards the School of Art, was 60ft longer than the other plan showed. The Railway Company also objected to the additional words in clause 2. After lengthy and sometimes heated discussions the Council finally decided to stand by their guns and insist on the alterations to the agreement they had already submitted.

The "Notes and Notions" column of the *Gazette* of 16th April 1901 carried a succinct summary of the position, which is worthy of full consideration.

"Bideford may as well resign itself now to a railway along the quay road. The Council may or may not have been short-sighted in assuming an attitude of benevolent neutrality towards the original Westward Ho! Railway Company when its Bill was before Parliament in 1895-6. Given the circumstances, and the knowledge that then obtained, one is inclined to doubt whether the Town Council as now constituted would have acted differently from its predecessor. But the conduct of later negotiations is more open to criticism. The original Railway Company disappeared, and the powerful British Electric Traction Company having a solid capital backing reckoned in millions, had to be reckoned with. The Council should have realised that the only hope of securing concessions was by friendly negotiation and mutual compromise. The Company had its Act, and could not be expected to renounce any of its privileges without a clearly defined quid pro quo. What has been the course of the negotiations? First the Council has threatened terrible things, then begged favours; resolutions have been passed at one meeting and rescinded at the next. Appeals have been made to the Directors to act the part of philanthropy, at the very time they were being denounced as thieves and sharpers. The natural result was that the said Directors believed the Council to be attempting to jockey them out of statute rights which the original Company were permitted to obtain, and for which, presumably, the new Company is paying, or has paid, in hard cash. Two can play that game, and thus we have seen the Company also trying to obtain concessions whilst evading responsibilities. At length, apparently, the Company decided to confine itself within the four corners of its Act of Parliament, and accordingly we find navvies are at this moment tearing up the Quay outside Trewin's stores, which is the termination of the line. One feels very mad at the wreckage of the one broad carriage way of which Bidefordians have been so proud, but it is as well to shut one's eyes, and wait until the road has assumed somewhat of its normal appearance. The occasional trains will be irritating at first, perhaps, but they will not be on the quay every minute, and the eye will soon become accustomed to them. This is merely preaching the doctrine of making the best of a bad business, but what else is there to do? The Town Council on Saturday did not feel justified in applying for an injunction to compel the railway to cease operations. The one thing on which one hopes the Council can, and will insist is that the rails should not be so laid as to cause the road on either side to fall away like an embankment. That would be a positive danger to vehicular traffic."

A few weeks later, the Council met to receive a new set of plans for the railway on the Broad Quay, with a request to sign them as agreed. It was stated that the plans had been drawn up for the protection of vehicular traffic as in clause 9 of the agreement. The Board of Trade had decided that Council permission was not required before the Railway Company had started opening up the roadway as the amendment to the plans was in the Council's favour. The Council approved and signed the plans. The meeting did however decide to draw up a statement of their points of opposition to the railway running down the Broad Quay in time for the forthcoming Board of Trade inspection. They also agreed to include their opposition to the use of steam power on the Quay in this statement.

The Town Clerk was instructed to write to the Board of Trade seeking a meeting at which they could put their views. The meeting understood that the railway was due to start running the following Saturday – 27th April 1901. However, the first formal running of the line took place on Wednesday, 24th April 1901 when, according to the *Gazette*, "a pleasant company assembled, at the invitation of Mr Sowden, the new Company's traffic superintendent, at Curtis's Marsh, (Author's note: the temporary terminus round the corner from the Quay) to take part in a preliminary run over the new line."

Interestingly, alongside the lengthy article describing the first trip, there was a short piece on an accident the previous week at Tralee station in the west of Ireland, when a runaway train had crashed killing the driver, fireman and guard. The article poses the picture of a runaway train of corridor (!) coaches travelling at 30 miles per hour along Bideford Quay and suggests: "there would be more than the driver, fireman and guard killed. And yet there must always be such a possibility. I trust such a contingency will not upset the nerves of the nervous ladies who perambulate the thoroughfare." Hardly the sort of comments the Railway Company would have wanted at such a time.

But to return to the afternoon of Wednesday 24th April when the sun apparently "shone in full splendour", the main article describes in glowing detail the proceedings as the locomotive *Torridge*: "decked with a Union Jack pushed two of the company's handsome carriages into position, and soon all who had accepted the kind invitation were seated. With a shrill whistle, and a locomotive snort, the train started off at a pace which would put to shame some of the big trunk line trains. The cheers of those assembled to see the company off had scarcely died away, when the chorus was taken up by groups along the line at the various level crossings."

After passing the Raleigh estate, the line entered the Kenwith valley and, passing North Down Hill, the line swept round to the right and climbed towards Abbotsham and Cornborough. Skirting the edge of Abbotsham Cliffs, the line then ran down into Westward Ho! The author of the article was clearly impressed by the scenery, for he waxed lyrical about his journey. Magnificent vista; tumbling Atlantic billows backed by the frowning cliff line; grand stretches of

Passengers get ready to board one of the inaugural trains. (Clive Fairchild Collection)

PLANS ARE LAID

The special train at Westward Ho! prior to the official opening. The station buildings were as yet incomplete. The well ballasted track is evident. (Chris Leigh Collection)

sand were just some of the phrases used. After passing the Nassau Baths and the Royal Hotel, Church and United Services College, the train came to rest "just opposite the Post Office, at the site of what will be the Westward Ho! station". After more cheering and good wishes were forthcoming, the train carried on past the Gas Works siding drawing up "at the Pimpley Road, the present terminus of the line, just above the palatial pavilion of the Westward Ho! Golf Club".

Photographing special trains was apparently in vogue even in those days and after a suitable photographic stop, the train made its way back to Westward Ho! for an hour's stop during which those who wished could bask on the rocks or stroll on the sands. During this period, Herr Grupp's band "which had accompanied the party from Bideford" (musically or just socially, one has to ponder?) "discoursed some excellent music". This event was certainly the epitome of an English afternoon, for: "as 4.30 approached, tea and its usual concomitants were served, the purveyor being Mr Galliford of Westward Ho! Needless to say, the refreshment was heartily enjoyed, and put one and all on good terms with himself and all the world for the short return journey. Bideford was reached about ten to five, all having spent a pleasant afternoon." This being the case, it would seem that not too long was allowed for tea!

The lengthy article continued by setting out the basics of the timetable and fare structure: the service to start at 8.00am and every forty-five minutes thereafter with fares at 5d (third class) or 8d (first class) for the single journey from Bideford to Westward Ho! First class fares were stated to be 8d single, and 1s return. Excursions at 6d return were to be run on Mondays, Wednesdays and Fridays, with bathing trains to operate in the season and form a feature of the Sunday traffic. "It is anticipated that an arrangement will be concluded with the London and South Western Railway Company for through bookings from the stations on the line to Westward Ho!" There then followed a brief history of events leading up to the construction of the line with mention being made of the "considerable controversy" between the Corporation and the Company.

A neat summary of the position regarding operations on the Quay then follows:

"The company wanted a loop line on the Quay, in order to reverse the engines, but they were unable to come to terms with the Corporation, and the line is now being completed as a single line. In working the traffic it will, therefore, be necessary to keep a spare engine and run this down to the rear of the train to make a fresh start on each journey. As there are to be two trains and three engines, there will always be an engine in reserve, and each of them will in turn draw the train to Northam."

THE BIDEFORD, WESTWARD HO! & APPLEDORE RAILWAY

(Northam was the actual terminus of the line at Pimpley Road, just past Westward Ho!) A detailed and most interesting description of the carriages and locomotives follows:

"Another feature distinguishing the line from most others is the construction of the carriages. These are built on the American principal (sic), with a central corridor, and are entered, like tramcars, from the ends, instead of the sides. The seats are reversible, and are nicely upholstered. Built in this manner the carriages are roomy, comfortably seated, well ventilated (all the windows will open), and abundantly lighted, and the change from the ordinary mode of construction is one which will be appreciated by passengers. Each coach measures 40 feet in length and has a width of nine feet, and they will seat 10 first and 40 third class passengers. Two coaches will make up a train. Polished teak has been used for the outsides of the coaches, while the interiors are panelled in polished oak, with teak mouldings, the roofs being panelled with white lincrusta-walton, picked out in gold.

"The engines are so cased in that the wheels and practically the whole of the machinery are invisible. Engines and carriages are fitted with automatic vacuum brakes. As the tickets will be issued by the conductors of the trains, there are no ticket-offices. The tickets, like some of the other arrangements, are after an American pattern. They are torn from a counterfoil book, which is so contrived that each separate slip will indicate the starting point and destination of the passengers and the amount of fare paid; the corresponding half, kept by the guard, bearing the same indications."

The article concludes by stating that the original contractor was Mr Chadwell of Blackburn who "transferred his interests to the British Electric Company". This is an interesting choice of words in the circumstances. From this article it certainly seems that many were in favour of the new railway and that future prospects were bright. Mr W.J. Gale was the resident engineer and Mr Henry Sowden the traffic superintendent, later General Manager. The latter was previously the stationmaster at Blackmore Gate on the Lynton & Barnstaple Railway, although the *Railway Magazine* noted his 13 years service in the traffic department of the Somerset & Dorset Joint Railway.

The *Gazette* of 14th May 1901 carried a short report of a council meeting at which criticisms were made of the way the railway was being laid along the Quay. After some discussion, the matter was left in the hands of the Surveyor. The article was followed by a letter from "Lookout" who also complained about the way the line was being built and hoped that the Council would make strong representations to the Board of Trade Inspector on his inspection which was taking place that very day.

Inspection and Approval

Colonel Yorke did indeed inspect the line on 14th May 1901 and his report to the Assistant Secretary of the Railway Department of the Board of Trade is dated 18th May and runs to 14 typewritten pages. The preamble notes "this is a composite undertaking, partly railway, and partly tramway, and possessing some unusual features…". Colonel Yorke deals firstly with Railway Number 3 (the short length from Westward Ho! then built) and the railway part of Railway Number 2 from the Pill to Westward Ho! Summarizing the report we see that:

- The line is single throughout, except for passing places at Bideford Yard, Mudcot, Westward Ho! and Northam.
- The permanent way is laid with steel flat-bottomed rail of 60lb to the yard.
- Sleepers are 9ft x 9in x 4½in to which the rail is attached with fang bolts, clips and dog spikes.
- Ballast is of broken stone "said to be" laid to a depth of 12in.
- The road is in very good condition.
- Steepest gradient is 1 in 40 and the sharpest curve is of 5 chains radius for a length of 1.74 chains at the point where the tramway joins the railway. A check rail is fitted. The proviso for minimum radius of curves to be 8 chains is waived as the line is to be operated as a light railway with a maximum speed of 25 miles per hour.
- Fencing was noted to be generally sufficient except in a few cases.
- The station at Westward Ho! is reported as having two platforms each 320ft long and 1ft above rail level. The buildings were not completed at the time of the inspection. Northam's station had a single platform 180ft long and 6in high "on which is erected a small shed". Colonel Yorke felt this provided insufficient accommodation and requested the Company build a larger waiting room and a convenience for men! Booking offices were not required as tickets would be issued on the trains. Name boards for the stations were to be fitted, with lamps if trains ran after dark. Clocks were not needed at the stations, but should be provided in the signal boxes.
- Stopping places, with small platforms, were planned at Chanter's Lane, Causeway Crossing, Mudcot passing loop, and "one or two other places".

Civil engineering works were mentioned, including a note that the deepest cutting was 32ft, and the highest embankment 22ft. Two underbridges of steel troughs on masonry abutments were also noted having spans of 10ft and 12ft respectively. Five culverts of similar construction were also mentioned. These works, and the cuttings and embankments were standing well and the bridges showed "hardly any perceptible deflection when tested".

PLANS ARE LAID

"Torridge" stands on the Quay with one coach with "Grenville" or "Kingsley" at the other end. Judging by the wooden steps and crowd, this is probably the occasion of Colonel Yorke's inspection on 14th May 1901. The locomotive is not yet fitted with cowcatchers or "suitable fenders to push aside obstructions" as required by Colonel Yorke. (Roger Griffiths Collection)

Seven level crossings over public roads are noted at which gates and gate-keepers huts were provided, except at Westward Ho! where the stationmaster had control. Chanter's Lane, Causeway Crossing and Mudcot crossings were protected by signals. The first two of these were covered by the same signals – one up and one down. Colonel Yorke objected to this as the crossings were only some 300 yards apart and insisted on each crossing being fitted with its own signals to reduce the time the gates would need to be kept closed against road traffic. The Chanter's Lane gates were to be re-hung with a clear 16ft between the posts.

Causeway Crossing had produced considerable local opposition and the Colonel met a deputation on site to discuss their misgivings. Support for a bridge was noted by Colonel Yorke, but he felt that this would be prohibitively expensive and decided that safety issues would be met be the erection of a raised signal box affording a good view of both road and railway. The box should be equipped with the means to operate the gates from inside the box, and signals should be erected in both directions. Colonel Yorke was critical of the arrangements then in force as visibility was limited and the gates were not interlocked with the signals. Several of the other crossings called for minor comment and various requirements were laid down in the report.

The signal boxes on the line were noted at Bideford Yard, Gas Works siding, Chanter's Lane and Causeway Crossing, Mudcot, Westward Ho!, Northam station and finally a ground frame to the north of Westward Ho! station. Various signalling and inter-locking requirements were made in the report.

Operation of the line was to be by train staff and tickets combined with the absolute block system. The Company had issued an undertaking to this effect and this was attached to the report as was a copy of the Rules & Regulations. Colonel Yorke accepted these arrangements.

Carriages and locomotives were reported upon and found acceptable.

Subject to the requirements laid down in his report, Colonel Yorke recommended acceptance of the railway for passenger traffic.

The tramway section was then covered, being (a) the short part of Railway number 2 and (b) the tramway proper on the Quay. Colonel Yorke notes the "difference of opinion" between the Company and the Corporation of Bideford with regard to (a) as to position and method of construction. The construction of this part of the line was noted as being rails laid on sleepers with the ballast flush, or nearly flush, with the top of the rails. "No guard rail is laid and no groove exists such as is generally found on tramways." Colonel Yorke did not consider a standard grooved rail suitable for this portion of the line and suggested that a special rail would have had to be employed. He noted that the land on which the railway was laid was waste ground and, pointedly not getting involved with the wrangling over interpretation, felt that this section was fit for traffic. A speed limit of 6 miles per hour was stipulated, reducing to 4 miles per hour on the 5 chain curve.

Turning to the tramway proper as laid on the Quay, Colonel Yorke noted that the rails and mode of construction had been approved by the Board of Trade and the Corporation. However, he found that the groove exceeded the prescribed one and five sixteenths of an inch, being up to 2in in places. He considered this dangerous and required alterations be made to meet the original specification. The points and crossing for the siding at the north end of the Quay failed to meet with his approval and alterations were required.

Noting that the south end of the tramway, from Trewin's stores to the end of the bridge had not been made as the Corporation had refused to consent, the report then notes that the passing loop planned in this section of line had been omitted. Provision was made in the Act for loops to be made in other places with the permission of the Corporation and the frontagers. This not being the case, there was only a single line between the Quay and the Yard resulting in either trains being backed up to the yard, or second engines being run from the yard to attach to the train. Colonel Yorke felt that the former practice was dangerous and the second increased the usage of the road. He noted that it would be to the advantage of the Corporation, the public and the Company if a loop line were to be laid as on the Broad Quay and he hoped that an agreement could be arrived at on this matter.

The Corporation had pointed out the lack of fenders and whistles on the locomotives as required by the Act and this was to be attended to. It was also a requirement for "a seat for the driver in front of the engine" and this had not been provided. Colonel Yorke stated that this was not desirable and suggested that the regulation be modified by changing the need for a driver's seat to that for a standing place for the fireman. This was to ensure maximum visibility for the crew whilst running on the Quay.

The report was critical of the side steps on the carriages and required that they be altered so as not to project beyond the sides of the carriage.

Colonel Yorke concluded by suggesting that a re-inspection would be necessary once the groove on the line had been rectified and the carriages and locomotives altered as required.

A letter with a copy of the report was sent to the Company on 25th May 1901, sanctioning the use of the line as provided for in the report.

A good view of Westward Ho! station and signal box before most of the buildings were erected. The vehicle on the right hand line appears to be the brake van. (Marilyn Hughes, Westward Ho! History Group)

Chapter 3

To Westward Ho! and Beyond

The Inspector Returns

In March 1903, Colonel Yorke returned to North Devon and carried out his re-inspection of Railway Number 2 and Tramway Number 1. His report of 26th March 1903 notes that the requirements in his report of May 1901 in respect of Railway Number 2 had been satisfactorily complied with, but makes no mention of Tramway Number 1. Presumably he did not wish to involve himself in the continuing wrangles between the Company and the Corporation. Most of these problems were sorted out by the 1904 Light Railway Order, which will be considered later.

The following week's issue of the *Gazette* was published on the day of the official opening of the railway, 21st May 1901. In a column headed "Facts and Fancies" the author, "Bird's Eye", wrote of the great interest shown in the official inspection by Colonel Yorke of the Board of Trade. Bird's Eye saw the day as "the final struggle between the opponents and the company, and from the remarks made by Colonel Yorke, it would seem that some alterations will be obtained". The first bone of contention was that of the gap between the running rail and the check rail being too great and presenting a danger to pedestrians and vehicular traffic as Colonel Yorke had stated. Next, attention turned to the level crossings: "the rallying point of all the opponents". The Colonel had decreed that the gates were to be kept closed to road traffic, except when required to allow vehicles to pass. He also required a raised signal box with full signalling protecting the crossing to be provided at the Causeway crossing.

Writing before the inspector's report had been received, the paper nonetheless assumed that the rails on the Quay would have to be relaid with the correct, narrower, gap for wheel flanges. There was also a question regarding the alignment of the line on the Pill, which appears to have deviated from the original agreement. The article then relates that on the previous Saturday (18th May) six trains were run up the Quay carrying a total of three hundred passengers. On the Sunday three ordinary and two special trains were run carrying one thousand passengers. "Truly a very promising

The first train at Westward Ho! showing the well patronised train and Herr Grupp's band. The locomotive is still not fitted with cowcatchers but these were apparently in place by the time of Colonel Yorke's second inspection on 26th March.
(Chris Leigh Collection)

THE BIDEFORD, WESTWARD HO! & APPLEDORE RAILWAY

A scene somewhere on the Pill, probably close to Strand Road Halt. The crowds would suggest this is also opening day which, judging by the parasols and shadows, was favoured with good weather. Note the home signal. (Chris Leigh Collection)

beginning" said the paper. The *Gazette* had seemingly written to the Board of Trade requesting a copy of Colonel Yorke's report but had been told that "it is not the policy of this Department to publish reports".

There has been some doubt in the past as to the actual date of the official opening of the BWHA, with Monday 20th May 1901 quoted as the date, but it would seem from this article that in all probability the date was Saturday, 18th May 1901. The article concluded "Yesterday *(Monday, 20th May 1901)* the various trains were also well patronised. The spirit of competition is already making itself felt, and Messrs. Dymond, Son and Blackmore yesterday placarded their *(horse)* 'buses with a reduction in fares." So the area was already seeing additional benefit from the arrival of the train.

Plans for the line to Clovelly were finally laid to rest when on the 28th May the Bideford & Clovelly Railway (Abandonment) Bill was before the House of Commons. It was found to have complied with Standing Orders and on 25th June the Bill was passed for its third reading, after which it came into effect.

On 11th June, the *Gazette* reported, rather vaguely, that the Council had received a letter from the Board of Trade regarding Colonel Yorke's report. No details were given although surmise of the contents mentioned the rails, engines, and carriages. The short article ends by suggesting serious developments, which might include the Council attempting to have the line stopped by the Technical School before it reached the Quay.

On a lighter and more charitable note, it was reported that on Thursday 11th July, a group of inmates from the local workhouse were taken on a trip to Westward Ho! and back on the railway free of charge. This merited a note of thanks in the *Gazette*.

Returning to the letter received by the Council, this may have been in connection with Court proceedings reported the following week, "Much interest was centred yesterday in the proceedings taken at the Bideford Borough Police Court by the Bideford Town Council against the Bideford, Westward Ho! and Appledore Railway Company, for contravening the Special Act." The case came up on 15th July 1901 and the five charges before the court were listed as:

- Using steam power on the Tramway No.1 without having made a contract for the paving and upkeep of the roadway, as authorised under section 38 of the Act of 1896.
- The engines were not fitted with:
    – a speed indicator,
    – a bell or whistle or other means of sounding alarm,
    – a seat for the driver in front, or
    – a fender for pushing aside any obstruction.

Problems on the Quay

Discussions had apparently taken place between the Town Clerk and the Company's solicitors resulting in an agreement to plead guilty to the charges and to a fine of 10/- for each offence. It was stated that the case "had not been brought with any idea of harassing the Company, but to see that the safety of the public was maintained by the Act being properly complied with". The offences were alleged to have taken place on the opening day – 18th May. The Court accepted this, and the Company was fined a total of £2 10s 0d.

In response to requests from readers, the *Gazette* published in its 15th October issue, the full wording of Section 41 of the 1896 Act relating to the Railway or Tramway No.1 and the Railway No.2 which as we have seen was designed to protect the interests of the Corporation with regard to the portion of the line to be laid as tramway. No other comment was included in the article and one can only conjecture that feelings were still running high in the town in this regard.

By 3rd December 1901, the *Gazette* announced that negotiations between the Corporation and the Company were about to be reopened on the vexed question of the line on the Quay. The Corporation was still trying to get the railway to end on the Pill before it reached the Quay, but allowing the use of a siding on the Quay. A loop line could be allowed on the Pill for running round purposes. The sting in the tail came in the end of the article: "If it were possible for the Company to give an undertaking that, within a specified and reasonably short time they would use electricity as their motive power, the whole difficulty would vanish, including the objection to the trains going over the centre roadway." The use of steam power seems to be the crux of the whole matter and it is very interesting to see the real fact behind the objections stated so clearly for once.

On 13th January the Bideford Council met to discuss the ongoing matter of the railway along the Quay. Before the meeting was an amended version of the proposed agreement between the Council and the Railway Company, last considered the previous March. The main changes were the

"Torridge" brings her short train into Bideford past the Perkins & Sons building. The railway company's office is just to the left of the locomotive in the Perkins' building. It appears to have a sun blind over the window. The fruit and flower shop is to the right of this under the first floor bay window. (Marilyn Hughes, Westward Ho! History Group)

THE BIDEFORD, WESTWARD HO! & APPLEDORE RAILWAY

Departure time approaches as passengers board the train in the middle of the Quay road. (Beaford Archive)

omission of the clause leaving the question of steam power for the Board of Trade to decide, and a watering down of the clause withdrawing all complaints: this was now worded "The Council shall withdraw any further opposition to the working of the existing line on the Pill, and the Company shall carry out all the requirements of the Board of Trade with reference to the same." Broadly speaking, the Council had not changed its position regarding the extension of the line onto the Quay or the wharf and the new agreement was hardly a basis for new discussion. However, after some discussion, even this agreement was rejected by one vote and further negotiations with the railway were ruled out. The Mayor was then petitioned to hold a public meeting in the town so that the matter could be given a proper public airing. This meeting was arranged for Friday, 24th January 1902 and was to be held in the Town Hall. Prior to the meeting, a leaflet – published anonymously – was widely distributed in the town, urging "fellow-ratepayers" to resist the encroachment of the railway on to the Quay.

In anticipation of the public meeting, the *Gazette* carried a lengthy article on 21st January 1902 setting out in a very fair and unbiased way, the advantages and disadvantages of the situation. These may be summarised as follows:
- The Council had refused by a very narrow majority to entertain a compromise with the Company.
- The Act authorised the Company to lay a tram line along the short Bank and up the centre of the road on the Broad Quay with provision for a siding.
- The Company had then proposed carrying the line towards the bridge and then across the river on a new curved bridge to join the LSWR near the Gas Works. This proposal was withdrawn in the face of strong opposition.
- The Company later agreed to a terminus opposite Trewin's stores to the north of the High Street.
- The revised plans accidentally omitted the siding.
- As already stated, the Act gave powers to construct a line on the Quay and early in 1900 the Company started breaking up the road in order to carry out this work. This was stopped pending negotiations.
- The Council then offered a loop line on the wharf side if the Company would give up their rights to use the Quay.
- Disagreements over responsibility for the quay wall were eventually on the verge of settlement, but then a faction within the council pressed for the line to end on the Pill and not venture near the Quay at all. This led to stalemate and the company began to lay rails on the Quay in accordance with the Act.
- The Board of Trade inspection found faults with the check rail gap and this was to be rectified.

The Council then declined to negotiate further.

TO WESTWARD HO! AND BEYOND

A single coach train sets out from Bideford past Blackmore's Auction Rooms. The camera is looking down the promenade towards the bridge, with the Broad Quay to the right of the trees and the wharf to the left of the bollards. (Tom Bartlett Postcard Collection)

The *Gazette* felt that the forthcoming public meeting was essential and urged all involved to reach an amicable compromise. It did however object to the use of steam power on the tramway sections. Finally, the article points out very clearly that it felt that the Council, whilst acting with the best intentions, had under-estimated the powers of the Company afforded by their Act, and had also over-estimated the objections to the line being transferred to the wharf side of the Promenade. The public meeting was apparently very well attended and discussion was quite animated and heated at times. Opening the meeting, the Mayor gave the background to the relations between the Town Council and the Railway. He explained that it was not generally realised that steam power was to be used on the Quay, nor the disruption that would be caused by digging up the Quay to lay the rails. The Council had approached to Railway to see if they would move off the Quay roadway and on to the wharf, which would cause less disruption, but after arguments about responsibilities for the Quay wall, negotiations were broken off.

The Mayor then asked the Rev T. Newton Leeke to propose a resolution. There were objections to this procedure, but after some discussion, the Rev Leeke was allowed to speak. He proposed that a poll by held in the town to seek the views of the inhabitants as to whether the railway should run in the roadway on the Quay or on the wharf side. Councillor Pollard seconded the motion, but was subject to some heckling by fellow councillors. A discussion then followed during which it was alleged that a letter in the *Western Express* had suggested a loss of trade to the town if the railway went on to the wharf and that another newspaper had misrepresented the facts of the matter. The matter of the change of the gauge of the line was also mentioned. The Mayor then advised the meeting that a petition had been received signed by 35 coal merchants and other interested parties "praying to the Council to compel the Railway Company to adhere strictly to the Act, and not on any account to allow the Company to construct its line on the wharf side of the Quay, as it would be fatal to the shipping interest of Bideford. (Applause.)" This point was discussed at length, with several speakers against the use of the wharf. An amendment was then moved by Mr J.J. Lamerton that if a poll was taken, the ratepayers should also be asked if they approved "of the efforts, thus far successful, of the Council to keep the Railway Company off the Quay, and to compel them to terminate their passenger traffic on the Pill, and shall the Council continue to strive to accomplish this end?" More

THE BIDEFORD, WESTWARD HO! & APPLEDORE RAILWAY

discussion ensued, which was quite heated at times. Alderman Narraway explained that the Council had spent nearly £15,000 on purchasing and improving the Quay over the years and it was a serious point to consider. Eventually the original motion was put to the meeting and was defeated by a large majority. "The result was received with prolonged and vociferous cheering." The meeting appears to have had little effect on the ongoing battle between the Council and the Railway Company and the railway continued on its way.

Digging up of the Quay roadway for laying the tracks continued, and at its meeting on 30th January, the Council called on the Railway Company to give an assurance within fourteen days that they would complete laying the line on the Quay and the Pill within two months. In the meantime, a Mr Phillips of Appledore had claimed compensation from the council for damage caused when his horse fell "on defective railway lines on the Broad Quay". The *Gazette* of 11th February reported that the council had replied disclaiming any responsibility. This had prompted an anonymous correspondent to pen the following lines.

THE RAILS ON THE QUAY.
When driving into Bideford town
Beware the treacherous rails laid down;
For 'the powers that be' have left you free
To break your neck on Bideford Quay!

The Railway has the upper hand
And can the Council now command;
So it's not the Council's fault you see,
If you break your neck on Bideford Quay.

But why, alas? Has Bideford town
Its ancient powers laid meekly down,
To give the chance to you and me
To break our necks on Bideford Quay?

Ye Bideford merchants, wake anew!
What is your Council coming to,
If visitors come your town to see
Then break their necks on Bideford Quay?

On Thursday, 10th April 1902 the committee appointed to deal with the Bideford, Westward Ho! & Appledore Railway Company reported to the full Town Council the results of a meeting held on Monday 24th March with Stephen Sellon, the Chief Engineer of the Railway Company. Mr Sellon had offered to take up the present line on the quay and to relay it as far as Trewin's stores as near the promenade as possible, so as to leave the remainder of the road available for traffic. In return for this, the Council would allow a 66-yard long passing loop to be made from the terminus towards the Technical School. The use of wood blocks on either side of the rails was to be discontinued and replaced with another

The position of the train in the centre of the road can be clearly seen, with the promenade on the right and the Quay or wharf beyond. (Beaford Archive)

material to be mutually agreed. In response to this offer Mr Sellon was advised that "there was no chance of the Council entertaining this offer, and the Committee arrived at no resolution on the matter".

Following the meeting of the 24th, Stephen Sellon had obviously given the matter further consideration with a view to reaching a compromise for a letter from him was now before the meeting. In this letter he reiterated the offer to move the line nearer the promenade, but stated that he would be seeking either Board of Trade or Parliamentary powers as necessary to construct the passing loop. He continued by saying that he could see no way that he could advise the Company to give up its existing rights and that they were about to put a different pattern of rail down on the Broad Quay to comply with the requirements of the Board of Trade inspection. He concluded by saying that in his opinion the only matter outstanding was whether the Council wished to line moved away from the centre of the Quay as he had offered. This was on condition that no objection be raised to the passing loop. After all this, the Council decided to take no action!

Little progress seemed to be made until July when the *Gazette* reported that on Saturday, 5th July the Railway Company gave formal notice that they intended relaying Railway No. 1 (the line on the Quay) and to make "a turn-out or loop-line" on the Broad Quay. Hardly surprisingly, the Council decided to oppose the construction of the loop-line and to appeal to the Board of Trade. In respect of the relaying, they intended to discuss further with the Company the line on the Pill. The *Gazette* sagely noted that without such a loop-line, Tramway No. 1 "will not only be expensive, but difficult to run". Thus the scene was set for the "battle royal" of the construction, when at about 6 o'clock on the morning of Sunday 7th September 1902, a gang of navvies began "to hack and tear up the roadway for the purpose of laying a loop-line".

Tuesday's issue of the *Gazette* was full of the matter, declaring that "matters have reached a climax, and war has been declared by the local Town Council". The *Gazette* notes that it is rather surprising "that the tension did not earlier reach an acute stage". The article continued by pointing out that the Company had the right to construct its line on the Broad Quay, a loop line was needed and the Council had refused to allow this even though the Railway Company was willing to compromise on the position of the line on the Quay. Work apparently continued throughout the day, and the Town Clerk was instructed by the Mayor to proceed to London at once and obtain an injunction against the Company. A special meeting of the Council on Monday morning approved this action. The full committee of the Council was empowered to take whatever action was required. On Monday evening, "several hundred men, women and children assembled on the Quay" in protest at the

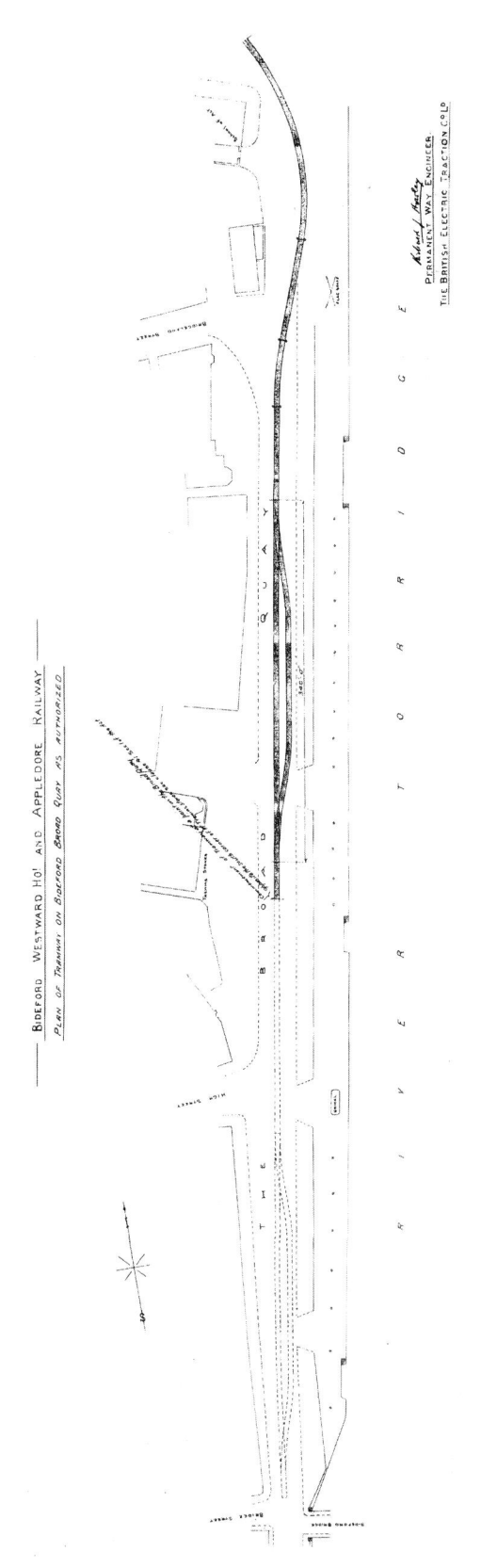

The revised plan for the layout on the Quay and loop line (June 1902), overlaid on the original plan. The siding is not shown for some reason.

49

THE BIDEFORD, WESTWARD HO! & APPLEDORE RAILWAY

Company's action in digging up the roadway. An orderly meeting passed a motion of protest against the Railway Company's action, and in support of the Town Council. It was also agreed that if the Railway Company did not fill in the excavations within 24 hours, the ratepayers would arrange for it to be done. The meeting then broke up quietly. The piece concluded: "At about the time of the meeting, the navvies stopped work."

By 16th September, matters were far from settled and the *Gazette* clearly felt that it needed to calm matters down by laying out the facts and the background to the railway for all to read. The article began by expressing the view that "had a more generous spirit been shown on the part of the town, there would have been no crisis and no unpleasantness at all". Sketching in the bare details of the incorporation of the railway, it continued: "no one ever regarded the undertaking as serious, even though the promoters had spent money to obtain the sanction of Parliament. Had a different view been taken of the affair, and had the Town Council only done their duty the present crisis would never have arisen, and a great deal of unpleasantness would have been avoided."

Originally, the *Gazette* reminded its readers, the intention was for a narrow gauge line right up the centre of the roadway to a point almost opposite the Bridge Buildings. To enable running round, a "turn out" or run round loop was to be placed. Later a standard gauge line was decided upon with the ultimate aim of connecting to the LSWR main line by way of a new bridge over the Torridge. Questions were raised as to the strength of the old Long Bridge as the new railway would have to cross at least the first span of the old bridge. Such was the opposition that the Directors withdrew the idea. The Council did not object to the proposals providing the Company did not erect any buildings on either the Pill or the Quay. It was agreed that the Company would not construct the line all the way to the Bridge Buildings without the final sanction of the Council, but due to a technical error, the loop line was omitted from the revised plan. Only the goods siding at the other end was left in. Once this was discovered, the Company offered to give up the line to the bridge and run along the wharf side of the Quay, if the Council would agree to a loop line. The Council were split on this and certain elements continued "their policy of obstruction".

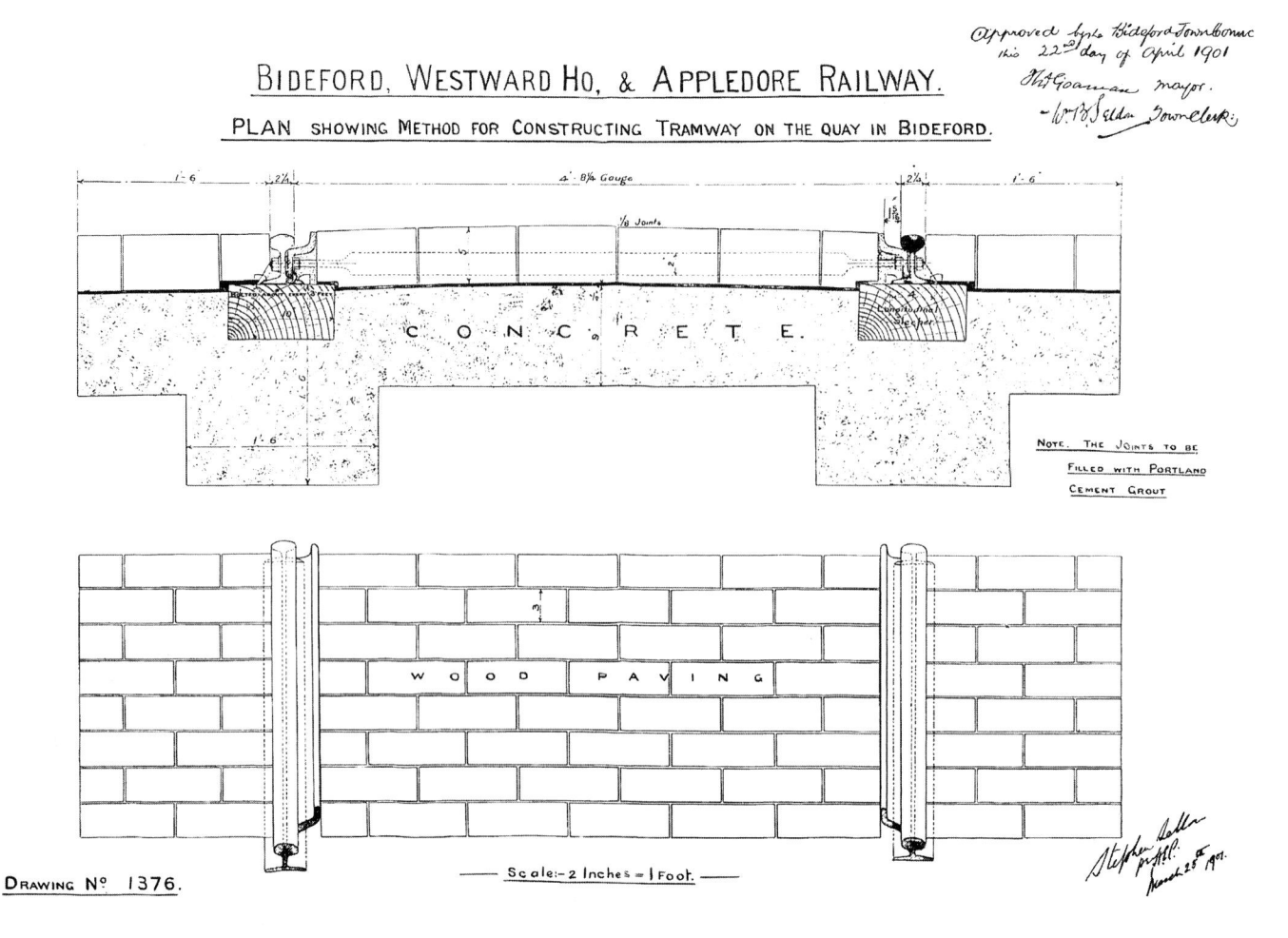

Plan showing the method of construction of the track on the Quay.

TO WESTWARD HO! AND BEYOND

Looking down on Westward Ho! from Kipling Tors. The tall signal protecting the station can be seen against the building near the water's edge. (Tom Bartlett Postcard Collection)

As we have seen, the Company eventually gave up on the Council and laid the line up the Quay according to the Act. The Board of Trade were not satisfied with the rail laid on the Quay, the gap between running and check rails being too wide, and insisted on replacement. Early in September, when the relaying was almost complete, The Company began digging up the Quay again to lay the loop line. The Council had issued a writ, but the *Gazette* interpreted the feeling of the more thoughtful members of the public as recognising the benefits of the railway to the town and being opposed to fighting the Company, which should be allowed to lay the loop line.

Page 8 of the same issue of the *Gazette* carried a note that, after consulting counsel in London, the Town Clerk had reported that it had been decided that it would be better to apply for a writ against the Railway Company, rather than an injunction. This apparently upset the local applecart, and a special meeting of the council was called for Wednesday, 10th September, upon the return of the Town Clerk. A separate paragraph on the same page commends the Mayor, Councillor Tattersill, for his strong stance at that meeting when he refused to accept a motion regarding the matter, which "practically amounted to an incentive to the public to commit a breach of the peace on the quay". The Town Clerk wrote to the Board of Trade on 18th September 1902 advising them that the Council had issued a writ in respect of the passing loop.

Meanwhile the Contractors were continuing with the excavations for the laying of the loop line, but the work was brought to a halt at about 7.00pm on the previous Tuesday evening by very heavy rain which "fell unceasingly". The previous day a public meeting had passed a resolution calling on the Company to cease work within 24 hours or they, the ratepayers, would fill in the excavations themselves. The deadline was 8.00pm on the Tuesday evening. At this time a large crowd had gathered on the Quay to watch the proceedings, but the contractor had spent most of the day loading the spoil into wagons to prevent the crowd using it to fill in their work. As the contractors had stopped work an hour earlier, the prospective militants were put off by their absence, and by the bad weather. The Chairman of the previous day's meeting was conspicuously absent from the scene on Tuesday evening having been warned by the Superintendent of Police that if the resolution he had signed was carried into effect "he might possibly see the inside of a local gaol". An enhanced Police presence on the Quay deterred any remaining aspiration to cause trouble.

A few weeks later, on 23rd September the Railway Company wrote to the Board advising that the loop had been laid and asking if an inspection was required by their inspector. The following day, a copy of a letter dated the previous day from Stephen Sellon, the Railway's Engineer in London, to Frank Ashby at the Royal North Devon Golf Club, Westward Ho!, was published in the paper. It would seem that the two men were close friends and in the habit of

THE BIDEFORD, WESTWARD HO! & APPLEDORE RAILWAY

A road locomotive (traction engine) and trailer cross the line on the level crossing at the eastern end of Westward Ho! Station. (Marilyn Hughes, Westward Ho! History Group)

discussing railway matters, amongst other things. The letter gives an interesting insight into the private thoughts of one of the top men of the railway. The letter ran,

"My Dear Frank,

"I have been exceedingly amused with your chatty letter, especially with regard to the late excitement at Bideford, due to my reconstruction of the present tramway lines, as well as the new passing place. I am glad to hear that you think the new passing place will be of great advantage to the undertaking, and also to the public who make use of the line. Does it not seem absurd to you, who have more than an amateur knowledge of tramway matters in general, that a Company should be placed in such a position, that a Council like that of Bideford could hope to obstruct them in doing their best to provide a system of communication between two places, which communication has been authorised by Parliament. It must be clear to the intelligent ratepayer that when Parliament sanctions a scheme between two places, it does so because the Promoters have shewn the highest authority in the land that such a connection is necessary to the public weal (wealth), and if that is the case, does Bideford for a moment imagine that Parliament would ever approve of the Corporation doing its best by a policy of obstruction by means of raising small technical objections to defeat the intentions and aims of the Promoters in improving the system for the public benefit, as well as trying to defeat the intentions of Parliament. The Corporation of Bideford does not seem to understand that a Promoter before he can obtain powers for the construction of lines has to show that the same will be to public advantage, and they do not seem to know, or understand, that Parliament has the power after the passing of such an Act, to force the Promoters to make such alterations to their system, and improve their service as they consider necessary for the public good. Now, a Promoter having obtained powers of this kind from Parliament is in the nature of a public servant, and he has therefore to consider his relationship to the public in that sense.

"To an old associate of mine in tramway matters like yourself, it is, as you say, an extremely interesting case, and it is for this reason that I have gone heart and soul into the matter, after the extremely unsatisfactory interview I had with the Bideford Corporation some time ago, when they pressed that I should personally go down, and after making that very long journey at considerable inconvenience, I was told by them that nothing would satisfy them, except the stopping of

Looking up Station Road and over the level crossing seen in the previous view. The fencing at the rear of the platform can be clearly seen. (Beaford Archive)

the line at the Pill. Everybody knows (yourself amongst the number) who use this line, what a great disadvantage this would be, and how absurd it would have been for me to have agreed to it.

"I hear that the Corporation have issued a Writ against the Bideford Company, and have done the same to the British Electric Traction Company. I therefore look with satisfaction to a very promising legal wrangle, which, if continued, will as far as we are concerned undoubtedly end in the House of Lords. Although such a fight would be exceedingly pleasing to me, who have spent a considerable portion of my life in upsetting the arbitrary veto sometimes exercised by Local Authorities, I am still hoping, however, in the interests of the Bideford Corporation, that wiser counsels will prevail within the minds of those who are responsible for the governing of the town, and the well-being of the ratepayers.

"I was exceedingly sorry that the few days I had with the grouse in Scotland prevented me from having the contemplated week at golf with you at Westward Ho! I should have liked to have gone round the old links again with you, receiving as before two strokes a hole.
Yours sincerely,
Stephen Sellon."

It is clear from this letter that Stephen Sellon was a determined professional who, had he been of that inclination, could have made life very difficult for the Corporation. As it was, he seems to have had a generous streak which hoped for reason to prevail to the benefit of all. And two strokes per hole! One assumes that Frank Ashby was, at least at one time, in the same business as Sellon and therefore understood the whole position.

B.E.T. Rallies Round

The owners of the Company, British Electric Traction, seemed quite pleased with its North Devon railway and the August 1902 issue of the *B.E.T. Monthly Gazette* carried an article on the line covering almost three pages as part of its series "Descriptions of B.E.T. Lines." A map of the area and some photographs illustrated a well-written piece describing the line, which then only reached Westward Ho! The article seems to have been written by the Company Secretary, S.R. Booth, and it is worthy of some investigation. Describing the run from Bideford, the article describes the start of "The Railway proper" as being the "Yard":

"...and it is here that the locomotive and car sheds are situated, while the local offices are not far away. The

A slightly fuzzy but interesting view of the Westward Ho! level crossing from above. The crossing gates are in the process of either being closed or opened. (Marilyn Hughes, Westward Ho! History Group)

locomotive shed is constructed of stone with a corrugated iron roof, and is large enough to hold four locomotives. It is provided with wooden troughs suspended from the roof over the centre line of the rails for the purpose of preventing the fumes eating away the iron; these troughs slope upwards and communicate with wooden chimneys by means of which the smoke is carried to the open air. Within the shed is a pit for the purpose of enabling the fitter to gain access to the machinery of the locomotives. The locomotives are three in number and are named 'Grenville', 'Kingsley' and 'Torridge' respectively. They are provided with speed indicators, and the wheels are cased in with thin iron plates for the better protection of wayfarers and vehicles on the Broad Quay. The car shed is a similar building and holds four cars, which are handsome structures of teak and have seating accommodation for ten first and forty third class passengers each, with the exception of one car which seats thirty third class passengers only, the rear portion being used as a guard's van. The cars are built on the American plan, with a gangway down the middle and doors at each end; they resemble the type of car used in Switzerland, a type very well adapted for scenic lines by reason of their large window space. In addition to this rolling stock there are a box van, two covered goods wagons and six open wagons."

After Chanter's Lane and The Causeway, the line "runs up the pleasant Kenwith Valley with its green fields and delicately tinted woods. For some distance the train runs along the bank of the Kenwith Stream which exhibits an unpleasant tendency to encroach on the railway embankment." We are assured that the stream is being straightened out here to avoid flooding. Steep gradients of up to 1 in 47 lead to Abbotsham Road which "is a pretty station in the midst of trees, and is provided with the half-way passing place". At Cornborough Cliffs the traveller is afforded "what is undoubtedly one of the most beautiful views in North Devon". Mr Booth waxes eloquently about the scenery and the views and continues by describing the facilities available at Westward Ho! station, including the nearby troupe of entertainers "performing twice on weekdays and once on Sundays during the summer months". The Company apparently engaged them to attract visitors to the area. The golf links at Westward Ho! are also highly praised. Mr Booth then justifies his longer than usual article by again quoting the scenery and the rich literary and historical traditions of the area. He quotes Kingsley's description of Bideford as we have done earlier. He continues by mentioning Bideford's old bridge which he says is "sadly modernised with a hideous superstructure of iron". Finally he advises that no length of description can equal a short visit to "this delightful corner of Old England".

The article concludes with some very interesting information and statistics, which are reproduced on the opposite page. Interestingly wagon numbers are not mentioned in the table and we see that the two third class coaches were not yet in operation.

TO WESTWARD HO! AND BEYOND

Bideford, Westward Ho! and Appledore Ry. Co.

Board –

F. W. Chanter, *Chairman*
Capt. G. M. F. Molesworth, R.N.   C. L. Robertson
G. R. Hulme
S. R. Booth, *Secretary*

H. Sowden, *Traffic Superintendent*

Authorised Capital –
  Share Capital: £50,000 in £10 shares
  Loan Capital: £16,666
Subscribed Capital –
  £46,810 in £10 shares
  £7,800 in 4% £100 debentures.
Powers of Company –
  Bideford, Westward Ho! and Appledore Railway Act, 1896.
Broad Quay Tramway – The Chief Engineer reports that the tramway will be relaid on the Broad Quay at an early date, and that he has succeeded in obtaining a rail which meets with the approval of the Board of Trade. – S.R.B.

EQUIPMENT and ROUTE MILEAGE DATA

	NUMBER	TYPE	TOTAL H.P.
Steam Equipment –			
Engines	3	Side tank Locomotives.	--
Cars	4	Railway composite carriages.	--
Wagons		Goods.	--

	MILEAGE		
	ROUTE	DOUBLE	SINGLE
Gauge 4 ft. 8½ ins.	5' 5	---	5' 5

EMPLOYEES

Clerks	1	*(Repairs)*	
Inspectors	1	Blacksmiths, Fitters	
Drivers, Firemen and Conductors	5	and Turners	1
Engine cleaners	2	Permanent Way Men	5
Bus Conductor	1		---
Signalmen	3	Total	25
Gatemen	6		

Period 1902	Car Miles	Passengers	Receipts
			£
4 weeks to 20 June	2,820	7,851	94
Corresponding Period	3,000	13,064	217
Total from 1st January	15,423	39,331	458
* *Corresponding Period*	3,710	16,757	286
Total for Year 1901 *(From May 18th)*	25,347	110,647	1,453

TO WESTWARD HO! AND BEYOND

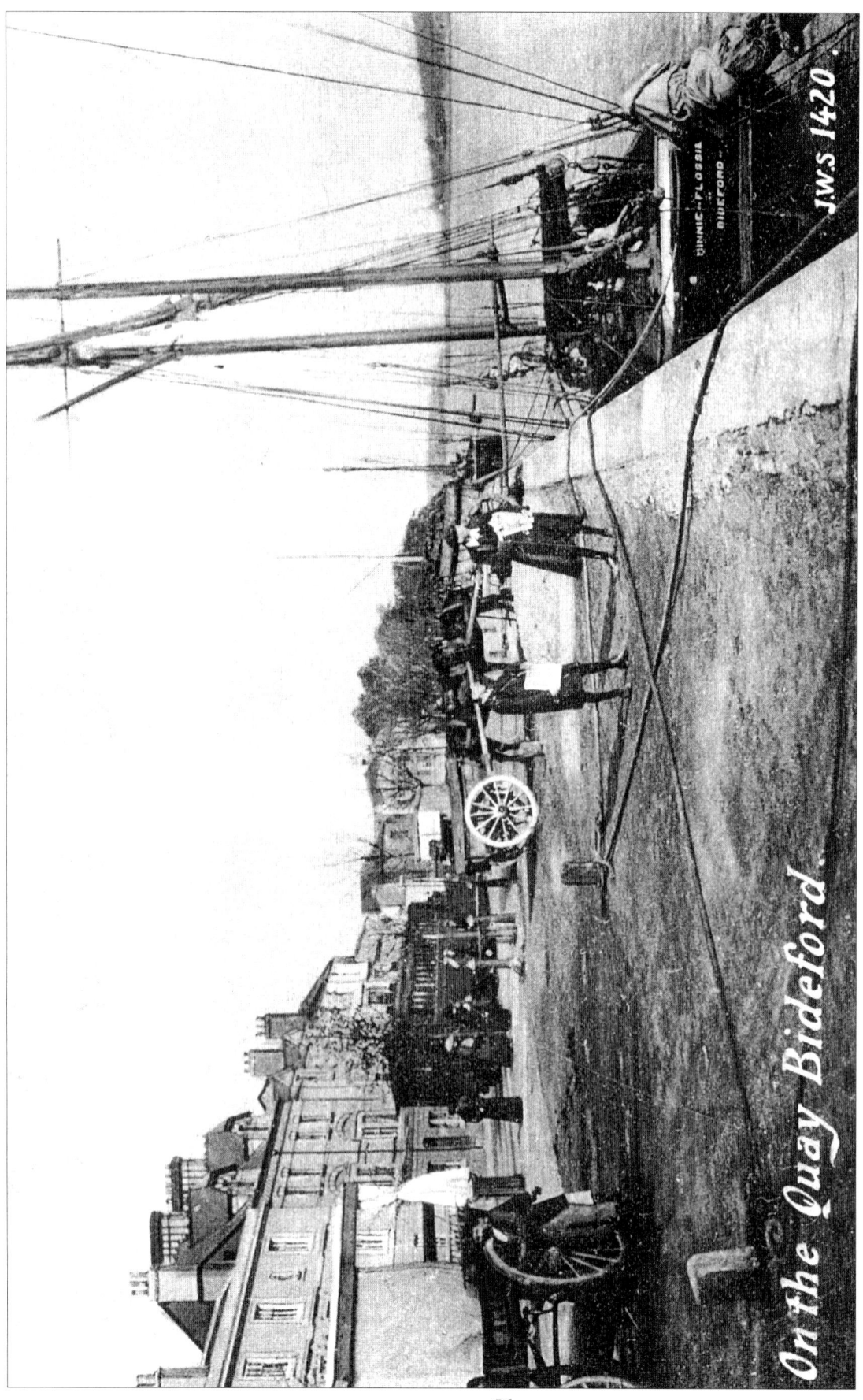

On the Quay Bideford.

A really lovely postcard view of the Quay from about 1906. Local boat "Minnie-Flossie" is moored up at the Quay being loaded or unloaded to the horse carts nearby. A train waits quietly on the Quay road for the "off". The scene hardly seems to justify the local opposition to the railway on the grounds that it interfered with the normal use of the Quay. (Tom Bartlett Postcard Collection)

Chapter 4

Operation and Extension

On to Appledore

As from 1st May 1903, the Company published the first edition of their *Official Time Tables and Guide*, price 1d, or 2d post free:

"It is a convenient handbook, and contains a number of good illustrations of Bideford and Westward Ho! a map of the district, and descriptive letterpress. An interesting outline of the attractions of Bideford and Westward Ho! is given, and an excellent description of the route covered by the trains. There is a special article dealing with the 'Submerged Forest' of Westward Ho! and the remainder of the book is devoted to timetables and general information useful not only to visitors but to townsfolk."

With the railway now in full operation from Bideford to Westward Ho! the owners and managers of the line turned their attention to completion of the original plan and formally announced the extension to Appledore. At an Extraordinary General Meeting of the Bideford, Westward Ho! & Appledore Railway Company on 16th June 1903 it was agreed to apply for a Light Railway Order to extend the railway. Stephen Sellon, the Company's engineer, presented revised estimates totalling £13,919 14s 0d in respect of the extension to Appledore. This figure included £750 in respect of electricity generating stations, etc. The *Bideford Gazette* devoted some space to the matter on Tuesday 26th May when it reported that the Company was proposing to electrify the existing line, and promoting "various extensions". The details reported were that the line was to be extended from Northam to Appledore, along the Quay at Bideford and a loop line to be installed on the Pill.

The extension to Appledore was enthusiastically welcomed by the *Gazette* which reported that local interests in Appledore were pressing for such an extension. The extension along the Quay was highlighted for "instant and careful attention, and possibly prompt and vigorous action"! The *Gazette* again puts the case clearly and unequivocally that the Council had allowed the railway to obtain its Act with little opposition and if it still objects to the line on the Quay, now was the time to act. "If *(the Council was)* successful well and good, if not there can be no subsequent heart burning or recrimination." The article goes on to say

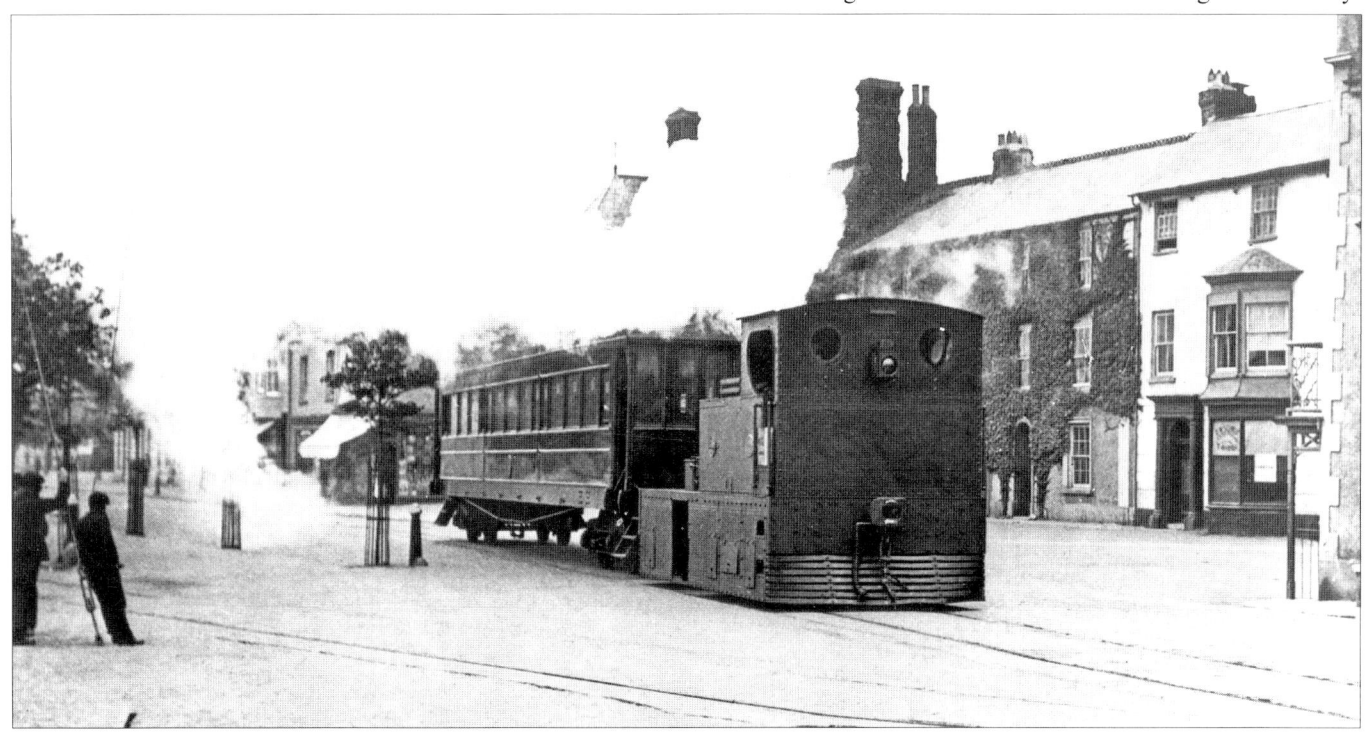

"Torridge" draws her train smartly out of Bideford past the goods siding. (Chris Leigh Collection)

THE BIDEFORD, WESTWARD HO! & APPLEDORE RAILWAY

Above and right: A well known view of the Company's offices on the Quay. The clock's inscription reads "Train leaves for Westward Ho! Northam and Appledore". The flyers in the window advertise Workmen's and Market Day tickets. One wonders if the smartly attired gentleman in the doorway is actually Henry Sowden the Manager, or one of his staff? The shop next door is Perkins the fruiterers and florists, from whom the company presumably rented its office. The poster in Perkins' window seems to be advocating the use of oranges instead of drugs to fight influenza. (Bideford Library)

Below: A view of a train in the loop on the Quay with a member of the crew proudly posing for the camera. Note the headlamp in front of the chimney. (Ian Pope Collection)

OPERATION AND EXTENSION

"Grenville" or "Kingsley" waits quietly by the trees on the Quay as passengers board for the next service down the line. A quantity of luggage (and a bicycle) is loaded as an elegant couple drive serenely by in their carriage. (Bath Photographic, Bideford)

that any action by the Council with regard to the extensions in Bideford also depended on the whether or not electrification was imminent. The Council's attitude must reflect the interests of the Town and the article points out that erection of a generating station could lead to electric street lights for the town, "which also would be a good thing".

At a meeting of Bideford Urban Council on Thursday, 28th May, the question of the use of steam again appears to have been paramount. The matter was referred to be discussed by the full Council in committee. Stephen Sellon, the Company's engineer had written requesting support for the Light Railway Order application. This was received with laughter! The letter was "treated with contempt" as the Council felt that Company were not adhering to its original agreement with the Council. It was agreed to oppose the Order, with the exception of the extension to Appledore. Clearly there was still no love lost between the two parties and little if any desire for compromise.

The battle between the railway and the council came before Mr Justice Farwell in the Chancery Division of the High Court in London on Tuesday, 7th July 1903. The *Gazette* of the following Tuesday printed a full and detailed report of the proceedings which resulted in a victory for the Council with regard to the loop line on the Quay, the Judge declaring the loop line illegal. This did not really settle the matter, for a stay of judgement was granted until after the hearing of the Railway Company's application for a Light Railway Order on 22nd July.

As a reminder, the line then terminated about halfway along the Quay opposite the offices of Pridham & Sons (formerly Trewin's Stores). Popular feeling locally seemed to be against extension of the line up the Quay any nearer the bridge, but in favour of the loop line which was seen as advantageous generally. The *Gazette* ventured to suggest that although many people would attend the inquiry, the alternative attraction of Bideford Regatta might prove too tempting for some!

As it turned out, "a large number of burgesses and others were present" at the Town Hall for the inquiry, which the *Gazette* duly reported at length. The main points for the inquiry were the loop on the Pill, the loop on the Quay (which of course was already there and had been ruled illegal in the recent High Court case), and the transfer of the whole line to come under Light Railway provisions. There were also some minor matters regarding crossing places and details of alignment at Long Lane in Northam which were being settled by negotiation locally. The hearing was clearly heated at some points with the question of the extension up the Quay and the loop line to the fore.

The root of the problem involved the Council's contention that the loop line on the Quay was a crossing place of the road which, according to the Act, could not be allowed without the agreement of the Council. If agreed, at least one third of the occupiers of property abutting the road could require a space of at least 10ft 6in between the track and the footway. Under the provisions of the proposed Light Railway Order this condition would be overruled. As noted earlier, Colonel Yorke had commented on the desirability of a loop line on the Quay to assist in the running of the line and this point was pressed home by the Company. Through bookings with the LSWR had been arranged and it was inconvenient to have to transfer passengers from the present terminus half-way along the Quay to the LSWR station. The

THE BIDEFORD, WESTWARD HO! & APPLEDORE RAILWAY

A post-1906 view of "Torridge" arriving in Bideford. The statue of Charles Kingsley seen in the right background was erected in 1906. Note that the fireman is on duty on the front of the locomotive to keep look-out as Colonel Yorke required. A passenger on the veranda seems keen to be in the photograph. (Chris Leigh Collection)

A postcard view of "The Quay and Light Railway". An air of unhurried leisure pervades the scene. (Beaford Archive)

OPERATION AND EXTENSION

Company provided a bus at a cost to it of £60 per annum. The fare was 2d which was disproportionate to the fare of 4½d from Westward Ho! The Company maintained that the natural terminus was the end of the bridge.

The opposition to the lines and loop on the Quay was strong and vociferous, although one speaker was in favour of extending to and crossing the bridge! Several speakers opposed the application altogether although seemingly just as many supported it. Prominent businessmen from Appledore were greatly in favour of the extension. It was stated that many of the men employed in the Appledore shipyards had to walk to work from Bideford each day and the railway would be of great benefit to them. Likewise about 60 girls from Appledore worked in the collar factory at Bideford and again these would benefit from the railway. Figures quoted during the hearing of 138,000 passengers and 1,500 tons of goods carried during 1902 suggest that the line was doing quite well in spite of the apparent opposition in some quarters. The Company felt that opening up to Appledore would increase revenue and profitability.

The Commissioners finally granted the Order, with the exception of the extension of the line along the Quay and towards the bridge. Thus the extension to Appledore was approved and the line was to be worked throughout as a Light Railway. The passing place on the Quay was approved as was the loop on the Pill subject to certain relatively minor conditions.

The decision of the Commissioners created a paradox in that they sanctioned a loop line on the Quay which had been declared illegal by the High Court only weeks earlier. The *Gazette* yet again got to the heart of the matter in its article on 4th August when it suggested that, as the line was actually in being and doing good for the trade of the town, a compromise should be reached whereby the line and its loop should be allowed, but moved to the wharf side of the Quay away from the main thoroughfare. Two strongly worded letters in the paper a fortnight later underlined the feeling against any compromise. One correspondent suggested forming a local syndicate at £1 a share to run a "motor break service" between Bideford, Northam, Appledore and Westward Ho! This, he stated, would be akin to the recent service introduced between Helston and the Lizard. The writer was obviously unaware that this service was run by the GWR as a feeder for its Helston branch line. In the meantime, the Company had been requested to remove the loop line from the Quay, but there was great fear expressed in Council that men would be employed on Sundays in "desecration of the Sabbath".

"Torridge" runs into the run round loop on Bideford Quay. There seems to be enough room for both railway and road traffic in this scene. (Tom Bartlett Postcard Collection)

THE BIDEFORD, WESTWARD HO! & APPLEDORE RAILWAY

Operation and Obstruction

In the meantime, as part of its plans to attract customers, the Company erected a hall on the station at Westward Ho! It had a capacity of 300 people and was built to provide a venue for entertainment and for use of the Company's passengers in stormy weather. The building was of masonry with a galvanised roof, was 96ft long and 25ft wide and was provided with a stage. The interior was finished with matchboard, stained and varnished. The opening performance on 2nd September 1903 was provided by the Bideford Black and White Minstrels. "A large number of persons attended." The Company was granted a music and dancing licence for the premises effective between the hours of 11.00am and 11.00pm.

At its meeting of 12th January 1904, Bideford Council registered its continuing opposition to the Light Railway Order. On Thursday, 21st April 1904 the objections to the Order were heard before Sir Herbert Jekyll, Secretary of the Railway Department of the Board of Trade in Whitehall. The objectors' case was that the provisions of the Act could not be overruled by a Light Railway Order and that the use of two engines between the Pill and the Quay was quite satisfactory. The Company's point was that the provision of a loop line was in the interests of safety and efficient operation and had been endorsed by the inspecting officer, Colonel Yorke. After much discussion and argument, the hearing closed and the Board's decision was announced later in favour of the Company; both loop lines – the contentious one on the Quay and an additional one on the Pill – being allowed. The matter was not allowed to rest, for the question was raised in Parliament by Mr Soares, the local M.P. He was advised by the President of the Board of trade that the matter had been through the proper channels and that the Board upheld the decision of the Light Railway Commissioners. It seems that the views of the Inspecting Officer were held in high regard.

On Tuesday, 28th July a special meeting of the Town Council had been called at the request of the Directors and Solicitors of the Railway Company to discuss transferring the line from the Quay road to the wharf side. The Council met privately prior to the Company representatives joining them. After lengthy discussion, the meeting voted by seven votes to six with two abstentions not to see the Company representatives. The Company representatives were "much surprised by this decision, which marks the climax of a series of disagreeable episodes". The Company did not take this lying down and the *Gazette* of 5th July carried a letter from

A superb postcard view of the Quay showing the promenade running between the wharf to the right and the roadway to the left. It would appear that the loop line is now in existence and "Torridge" will shortly draw forward and run round her single coach train ready for a return journey a little later. The trees are beginning to bring a sylvan touch to the scene.
(Tom Bartlett Postcard Collection)

OPERATION AND EXTENSION

"Torridge" again on the Quay, this time having arrived with a two coach train. The fireman is presumably getting down to uncouple the engine. (Tom Bartlett Postcard Collection)

A train on the loop awaits departure time. The lady and little girl on the left walk past unconcerned. (Bideford Library)

THE BIDEFORD, WESTWARD HO! & APPLEDORE RAILWAY

A striking portrait of "Torridge" having just arrived with one coach on the loop line, with what appear to be several Company men in attendance. On the right, the fireman has just removed the lamp from the front of the locomotive. The driver is on the footplate. The conductor with his ticket machine stands alongside the coach and in the four-foot another member of the staff walks towards the end of the loop, point lever in hand, to change the points for the locomotive to run round the coach. Two other staff members look on to the left of the picture. Just above the head of the flat-capped man on the left can be seen the clock sticking out from the wall of the railway's office. Charles Kingsley's statue is seen in the distance.
(Chris Leigh Collection)

the Mayor attaching a letter he had received from the Company's solicitor expressing their regrets at not being able to meet with the Council and setting out the railway's views with regard to transferring the line to the wharf side of the Quay.

The Company's proposals were similar to those previously discussed which stated that they would remove their line to the wharf side of the Quay (the Council to make good the roadway), install a loop line and construct a waiting shelter on the Quay. The Council to provide facilities for a loop line on the Pill if this was to be required, and to support the Company's application for these works to the Light Railway Commissioners. Whilst firmly worded, the letter did offer the opportunity for the two parties to come together for the common good and left the onus of responsibility with the Council.

This letter was followed by one from Councillor Lamerton who was at pains to explain that the Council had, only a week before, declined to meet the Company but that one or two councillors had met privately with the Railway Authorities to discuss the matter! Clearly the Council was still divided on the issue. This generated an indignant follow up letter from Councillor Heard who confessed to being one of the councillors in question and regretted the missed opportunity of a further attempt to come to some agreement over the siting of the line. Councillor Lamerton was quick to respond pointing out what he saw as his colleague's errors of fact regarding what was and was not agreed in Council. This minor public bickering does not appear to have had any effect on the eventual outcome of the railway's position on the Quay.

OPERATION AND EXTENSION

A good view of the end of the Quay with the Art School on the left, Kingsley's statue to the centre and the bandstand in between. The flagstaff stands sentry on the right. The "main" line sweeps off to the left, while the photographer is standing in the "four foot" of the goods siding. (Tom Bartlett Postcard Collection)

A slightly closer view of the same scene with a train arriving from down the line. The guns in front of the Art School are referred to as the "Armada Guns" as they were thought to have come from Spanish ships wrecked off the coast in 1588 whilst escaping after the defeat at the hands of Drake and his men. This theory has subsequently been held to be false. (Tom Bartlett Postcard Collection)

THE BIDEFORD, WESTWARD HO! & APPLEDORE RAILWAY

The Company clearly lost no time in acting on the Order, for on 17th December 1904, Major J.W. Pringle R.E. visited Bideford on behalf of the Board of Trade to inspect the new loop line that had been laid on the Quay. His brief report advised that the new loop line on the Quay was 110 yards long and formed part of Railway No.3 under the 1904 Light Railway Order. Noting that the loop was to be used for passenger traffic and to enable engines to run round their trains, that the points were worked by hand, and that the permanent way was in a satisfactory condition, Major Pringle recommended that subject to a speed limit of 4 mph, the new light railway should be authorised for passenger traffic.

As a change from wrangling with the Council, the Railway Company seems to have been in discussion at this time with the Inland Revenue regarding the question of passenger duty. This was a tax levied nationally on the railway companies on every passenger they carried. It had been amended in 1844 to exempt those passengers travelling at special cheap fares. The Company had submitted to the Revenue that their fares met the criteria in the Act and they should be exempt. The Assistant Secretary to the Inland Revenue wrote to the Company on 9th December 1904 under the heading of the 1904 Light Railway Order, advising that "as there appears to be some doubt as to the actual effect of this law...and as to the intention of the Light Railways Act, 1896, the Commissioners will regard the Bideford, Westward Ho! and Appledore Railway as not liable to Passenger Duty subsequent to the date of the above Order". So at least the Company achieved a victory on this score.

On Wednesday, 22nd February 1905 Major Pringle was back in Bideford to enquire into the matter of replacing certain crossing gates with cattle guards. These were at Kenwith Road, Puse Hill, and Abbotsham Road in Northam, and Gas Lane and Hangers Lane in Westward Ho! A trial cattle guard had been erected on one side of the crossing at Kenwith Road and this was duly inspected by Major Pringle and the delegations from the Company and the various councils concerned. The council's thoughts were that the views of the level crossing from the road were quite restricted in places and that the guards were insufficient and would not

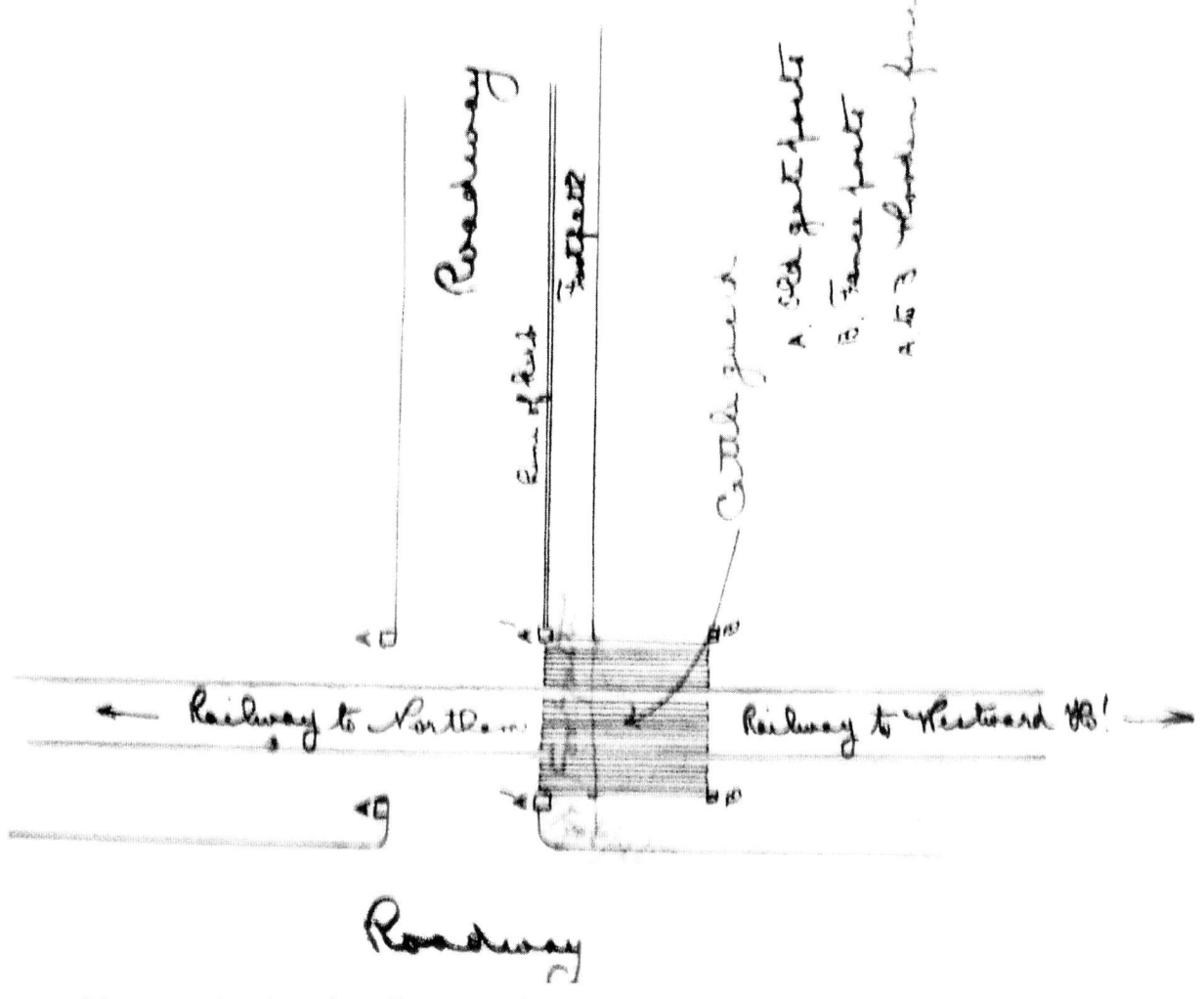

A drawing of the proposed cattle grid installation to replace gates at various crossings.

OPERATION AND EXTENSION

prevent children trespassing on the line. Mr Chanter for the Company expressed the view that even fences would not deter children. Major Pringle advised that he would be reporting to the Board of Trade promptly with his decision. In his report, Major Pringle firstly required a change from timber to angle iron for the slats of the guards and detailed the method of construction. Various other requirements were made for additional speed and caution boards to be erected at the side of the line on the approaches to some of the crossings and also that trains should stop at some of the crossings to reduce the danger to traffic and pedestrians. Major Pringle also pointed out that the Company should ensure good visibility from the road, by regular clipping and cutting of hedges. Subject to these requirements, he accepted the substitution of guards for gates.

On 9th September the Major returned to check that all these alterations had been carried out as per his instructions. He was apparently satisfied and, noting that in the absence of local representatives he assumed no further objections remained, he recommended authority to the Company to remove the gates now superseded by the guards.

In September 1905, the Company inserted a notice in the press that the gates at: "Kenwith, Puse Hill, Abbotsham Road, Gas House Lane and Beach Road will be REMOVED at 8.00am on Thursday next, September 21st 1905. The Public are requested to keep a sharp lookout for approaching Trains when crossing the railway."

The *Gazette* of 24th October 1905 carried a report that the Board of Trade had issued the Light Railway Order authorising the extension to Appledore, and the two disputed sections on the Pill and the Quay which had already been laid.

A fascinating development took place in 1906 when The Hunslet Engine Company was asked to prepare a design and detailed specification for a 21-seat steam railcar for the railway. The plans are still extant and Don Townsley's drawing taken from these is shown on the next page, along with an extract from the seven page specification. Regrettably, the project came to nought, but if the plans had gone ahead it would have produced what would have probably been the very first steam railcar of its type. With a seating capacity for only 21 passengers, one can only assume that the idea was to use such a vehicle during the quiet winter months when passenger numbers were low. Provision was made in the specification for towing a "trailer car" weighing up to 6 tons. This would have restricted its use to towing one or two wagons or vans. If the Company had actually ordered such a vehicle, some modifications would have been needed. The wheels and motion would have had to be covered as they were on the locomotives. Altered steps would be required to allow access from the low, or non-existent, platforms. Quite why the project did not proceed is not known, but a few years later the Company was again looking into the question of a self-propelled railcar, as we shall see.

During 1906 and 1907, the line continued to settle into its role and, especially during the summer months it would seem that traffic was quite reasonable. Details of traffic expenses and mileage run for the 6 months to 31st December 1906 show a total outlay of £367 5s 5d for the period, broken down as shown below:

Traffic expenses and mileage			
	£	s	d
Salaries and Wages	256	4	0
General Stores	7	16	3
Stationery, Printing, etc.	14	13	6
Tickets	3	10	6
Punch Hire		18	10
Running Bus Service	51	18	0
Licences	1	10	0
Water and Gas	6	12	3
Services of Minstrels	17	9	7
Clothing	6	7	6
Total	**£367**	**0s**	**5d**
Mileage – Passenger trains:	21,310 miles		
Mixed trains:	85 miles		
Total	**21,395 miles**		

Whether overall profitability was acceptable is another matter; on the above figures it would seem a close run thing, but B.E.T. was seemingly content to let the railway continue in operation.

The Company pressed on with the extension to Appledore and it is assumed that construction was again in the hands of Dick, Kerr and Co. The line ran across largely open country and construction must have been fairly straightforward apart from at the new terminus in Appledore, where four or five houses had to be demolished.

The month of April 1908 seems to have been of mixed fortunes as far as the weather was concerned for Easter Sunday that year apparently brought snow to London followed by rain which continued "until the empty, desolated streets ran small rivers" followed by more snow! Bideford however had a sunny but cold holiday weekend. "Excursionists to Westward Ho! however found the weather conditions there quite genial." Traffic on both the LSWR and Bideford, Westward Ho! & Appledore was hardly up to normal for the Easter period.

The work on the extension to Appledore was completed sufficiently by April for Major Pringle, who must have started to feel quite at home in North Devon by this time, to

THE BIDEFORD, WESTWARD HO! & APPLEDORE RAILWAY

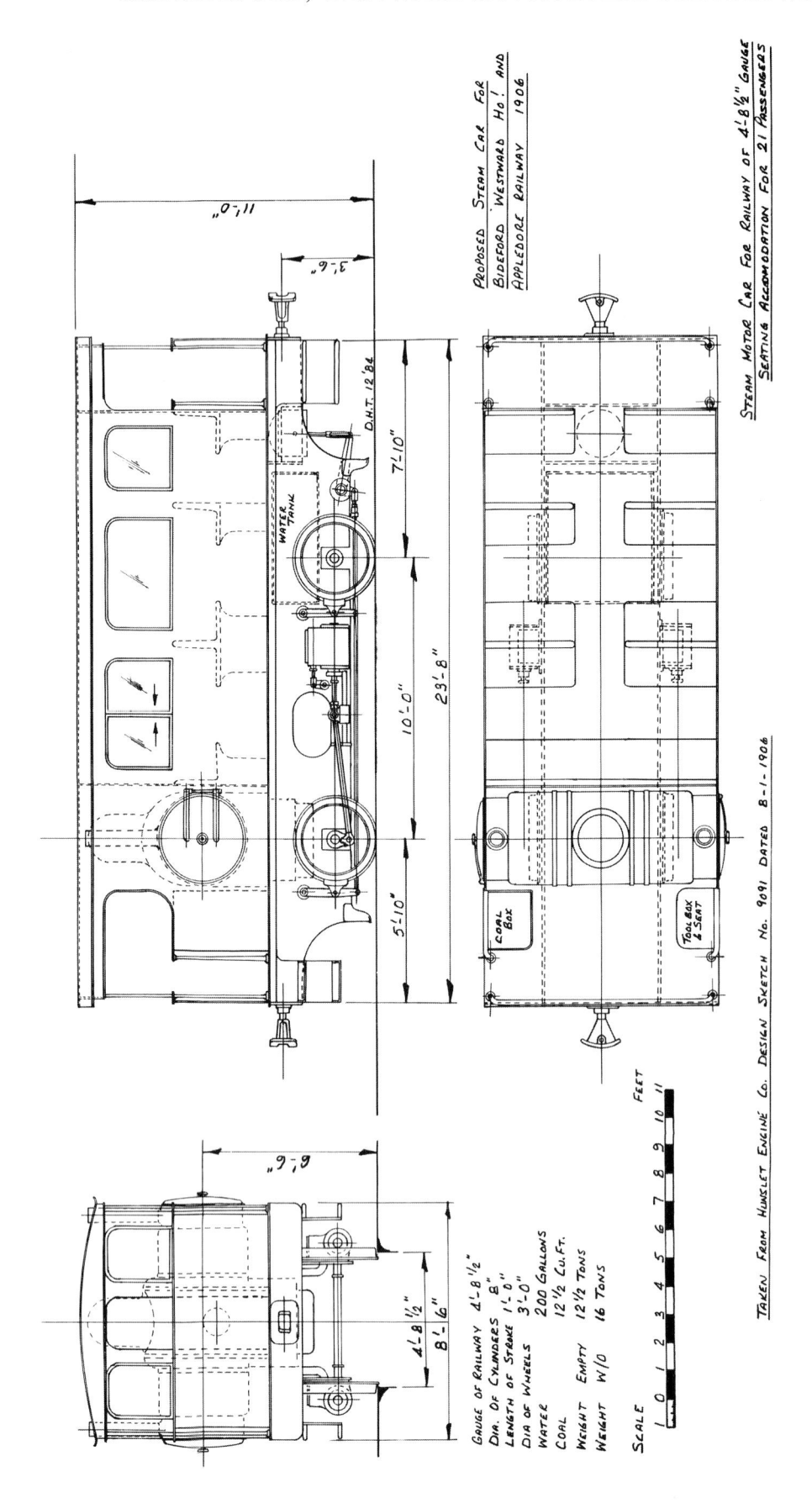

Donald Townsley's drawing of the proposed steam railbus, taken from the original drawings.

OPERATION AND EXTENSION

SPECIFICATION for a Steam Motor Passenger Car for a Railway 4ft 8½in Gauge

General Arrangement
The car and motor to be arranged generally as shewn in the accompanying tracing No. 9091.
It is to be complete and self-contained, carried on four wheels 3ft 0in diameter. Wheel base 10ft 0in. The cylinders to be 8in diameter x 12in stroke, placed outside of frames and actuating one pair of wheels. The motor and boiler compartment to be placed over the driving wheels. The passenger compartment to be entered at the other end and provide seating accommodation for 21 passengers.
The feed water tank to be placed under the footplate and between the frames.
The motor is to be capable of hauling, in addition to its full load of 21 passengers, a trailer car weighing 6 tons loaded, up gradients of 1 in 40 at a speed of 25 miles per hour, and of traversing curves of 3½ chains radius at 6 miles per hour.

Boiler
The boiler to be of the double-ended type, having a central fire-box and two short barrels, one pointing to each side of the engine and fitted with horizontal tubes.

Smokeboxes
There is to be a smokebox at each end of the boiler and formed out of the barrel plate and fitted with a circular dished door, opening on hinges to the side, giving easy access to the tubes for cleaning, repairs, &c. A chimney is to be fixed direct on each smokebox and carried up straight through the cab roof.

Frames
Each frame to be machined out of solid mild steel plate ⅝in thick extending from buffer beam to buffer beam, and well stayed together transversely by plates and angles.

Buffer Beams
To be made of steel plates ⅝in thick, well stayed to the frame ends by plates and angles.

Buffing & draw gear
Each beam is to be fitted with a strong combined central buffer and drawbar having link & pin coupling, solidly forged heads 18in by 12in cast steel guides, and steel volute springs. Height from top of rails to centre of buffer 3ft 6in.

Wheels & axles
All the wheel centres to be of cast-steel and fitted with Siemens steel tyres 3ft 0in diameter on tread 5in wide and 2½in thick. Centres of coupled wheels 10ft 0in.

Brakes
The car to have a powerful brake worked by a hand lever and screw through a pillar on the fireman's side of the footplate, also the automatic vacuum brake controlled by a patent drivers valve. The vacuum and hand brakes to be applicable either together or independently, and to act on all the four wheels through cast iron blocks, which bear on the flanges as well as the tread of the tyres. The vacuum brake to be also workable from the vestibule end of the car.

Cylinders
The cylinders to be 8in diameter and 12in stroke; of strong close cast iron, as hard as can be machined, to be carefully fitted and bolted to the outside of the frames by turned bolts in rhymered holes.

Valve motion
To be of the radius link type (that is, Stephenson – Author), worked by eccentrics on driving axle and connected by rocking shafts through the frames to the outside valve chests.

Tanks
To be made of steel plates and angles, and placed under the footplate between frames. Total capacity 200 gallons.

Fuel box
To be made of steel plates and placed on the fireman's side of the car. Total capacity 12½ cubic feet.

Cab & passenger compartment
To be made of mild steel plates ⅛in thick riveted together and stiffened by angles and battens.
The driver's cab to be open at the sides and above the handrail at the back. A division plate is to separate the boiler compartment from the passenger's compartment, which is to be entered from the vestibule at the other end as shown. The Hunslet Engine Co are not to provide the seats, (which are shown on tracing No 9091, only to indicate their arrangement), ventilators, lamps for passenger compartment, wood flooring, glass windows or frames, but are to provide the steel structure with all holes cut or drilled ready for the above mentioned fittings.

Control at vestibule end
Provision shall be made so that when the car is running vestibule end foremost, the conductor shall be on the lookout, and by means of an electric bell signal to driver in boiler compartment. A valve for applying the vacuum brake, and a cord to the steam whistle are also to be provided in the vestibule end.

Sandboxes
To have four sandboxes, two on each side, fitted with valves worked from driver's footplate, and pipes conduct the sand to the rails in front of the wheels at each end.

Painting
The car to receive throughout not less than two coats of plain colour in oil, to be filled up, rubbed down, and finally finished in olive green, or other such colour as may be desired, lined out, panelled, and varnished.

SUMMARY

	ft	in
Gauge of Railway	4	8½
Diameter of Cylinders	–	8
Length of Stroke	1	0
Diameter of Wheels	3	0
Length of Wheelbase	10	0

Capacity of Water Tank:	200 gall
Capacity of Fuel Space:	½ cubic ft
Working Pressure:	140 psi
Tractive Force at Periphery of Wheels:	2,130 lb

HEATING SURFACE
226 Steel tubes 1⅛in outside

Diameter:	203 sq ft
Fire-box (above bars):	36 sq ft
Total Heating Surface:	239 sq ft
Area of Fire Grate:	6 sq ft
Weight of car in full working order and 21 passengers about:	16 tons
Weight of car empty about:	12½ tons

Messrs
   The Bideford, Westward Ho! &
   Appledore Railway Co. Ltd.,
   BIDEFORD

THE HUNSLET ENGINE CO. LTD.
HUNSLET ENGINE WORKS
LEEDS.

January 28th 1906

THE BIDEFORD, WESTWARD HO! & APPLEDORE RAILWAY

inspect the line on 23rd April 1908 and his report dated the following day makes for interesting reading.

After setting out a brief description of the line, the report comments on the sharp curvature of the new extension and the fact that there are several places where reverse curves exist. Check rails were provided where necessary. "The earthwork is light in character and nowhere exceeds 7 feet in depth of cutting or height of embankment." Mentioning the footbridge at Appledore as being only bridge on the line – the report notes that no midway landing is provided even though the bridge height exceeds 10ft. However in view of the fact that "crowding is unlikely, this particular requirement may I think be waived". The report continues noting that no viaducts, tunnels or culverts of over 5ft in diameter exist. Fencing was noted as being acceptable. Following his previous recommendation with regard to additional warning boards at level crossings, Major Pringle also requires these on the new extension line. As to the permanent way:

"The rails used are chiefly double headed second hand steel rails, weighing 80 lbs per yard. These rest on cast iron chairs 40 lbs in weight, which are secured to second hand sleepers 9' by 10" by 5". Broken stone ballast, laid to a depth of 15" under the sleepers, is used. I noticed that at various places the top ballast was somewhat insufficient in quantity. This should be remedied. At the terminus (Appledore) and near the commencement, single flanged rails 60 lbs per yard are used. These rails are secured by a sufficiency of through bolts and clips to the sleepers."

Small platforms, about 1 foot high, were noted at Richmond Road (with a small shelter) and Lover's Lane (no shelter). The requirement for some form of lighting was noted "if used after dark".

At the new terminus of Appledore a single 300 foot long platform was provided with a small booking office, a general and ladies waiting room and "conveniences for both sexes". A run round loop was provided and the Major noted that a trap point was needed at the fouling point with the platform road. Home and starting signals had been installed and ground signals were to be installed. A 10-lever signal box was also provided and the Major made stipulations regarding interlocking between subsidiary signals and the points at the entry to the station. As the sighting distance of the home signal controlling the entry to Appledore station was less than the ¼ mile required in the Schedule to the Light Railway

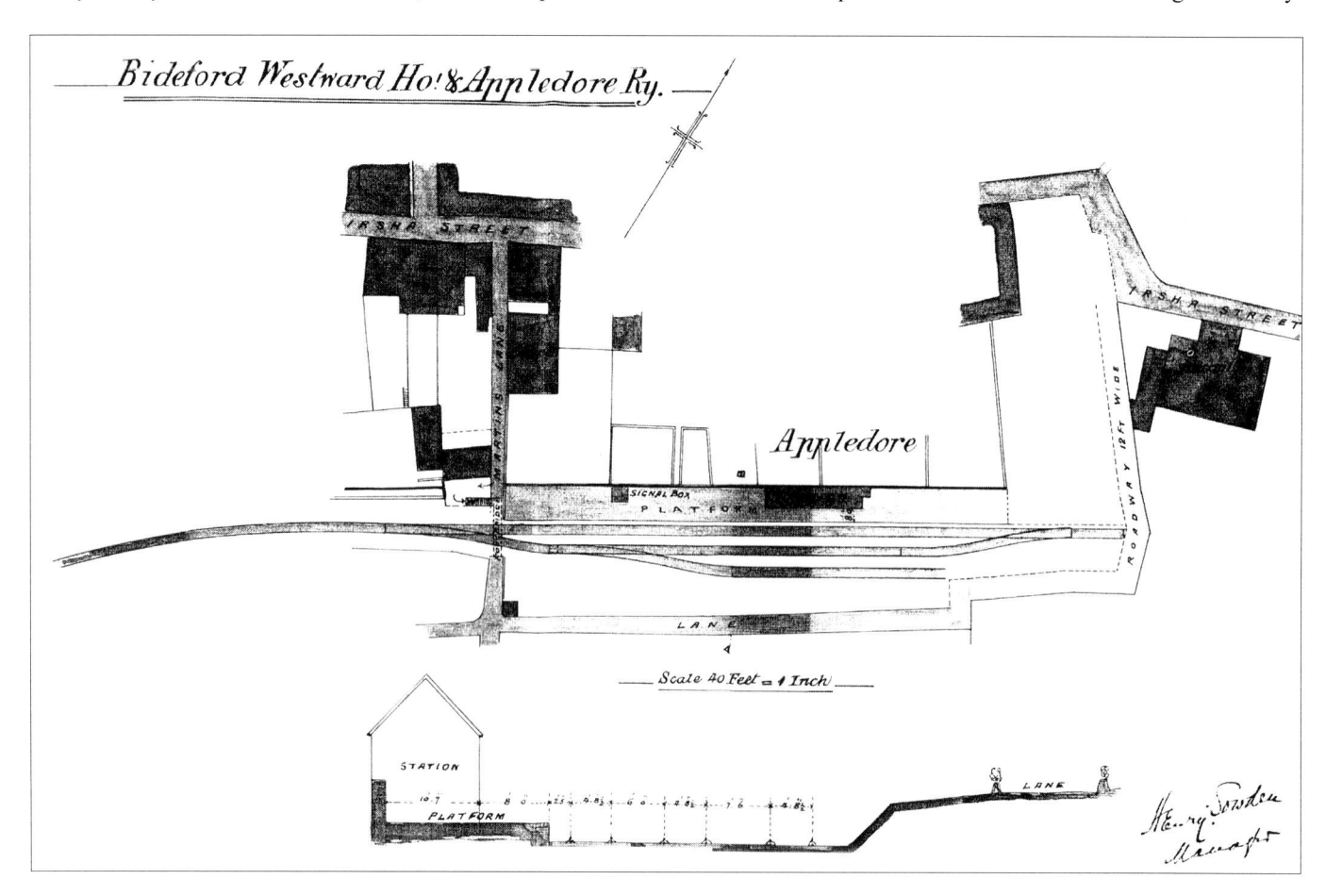

The layout of Appledore station showing the track, buildings and immediate area.

OPERATION AND EXTENSION

Order, he also made a requirement for a distant signal to be installed to the rear of that home signal at least ¼ mile from the station. "The new extension is to be worked by the train staff and ticket system, trains being signalled by telephone." The old section from Westward Ho! to Northam would be extended to Appledore, so that there was no additional section. At Northam, where the line previously terminated, the loop and siding points had been removed and there only remained a single line with no points or signals. Subject to completion of his requirements, the Major recommended approval of the extension.

"Thursday, April 23rd, witnessed the consummation of the Bideford, Westward Ho! and Appledore Railway, when the Board of Trade inspection of the extension of the railway from Northam Station to Appledore town took place."

Thus began a descriptive article in the *Gazette* which sang the praises of both the new railway and the countryside through which it passed, noting various local historical connections.

A full complement of passengers apparently travelled in the first train along the line which had cost, according to the paper, "something under £10,000 and the total expenditure on the line has been almost £80,000". The arrival of the train at Appledore was greeted by Mr H.R. Moody, the new stationmaster whilst the new platform, new footbridge and other available spaces were "crowded with interested sightseers. At the Public Hall in Irsha Street a large number were (sic) entertained at tea by the company and the Rev. G. Scholey proposed 'Success to the Bideford Westward Ho! and Appledore Railway'." Several speakers voiced their support for the railway which they hoped would be a great success. It was noted that not all the landowners had been helpful in assisting with the purchase of land, but eventually the land had been acquired. "After tea numbers of Appledore people were taken to Westward Ho! and back in one of the new sixty-feet coaches."

Major Pringle returned to Appledore on 18th September 1908 to confirm that his recommendations had been carried out. His report notes that four of these had been subsequently waived: the painting of cattle guards, the lengthening of some guards, automatic lighting at the two new platforms and the trap points and inter-locking in Appledore station. With these provisos, he recommended final acceptance of the new extension.

In time for the holiday season of 1909, the Company announced the opening, on Whit Monday, 31st May, of a new "HALTE AT CORNBOROUGH (for Abbotsham Cliffs)". Trains would stop to pick up or set down passengers on a daily basis "During daylight". Passengers wishing to alight should "inform the conductor on the train". Fares were to be "as to and from Abbotsham Road". The "Halte" was

BIDEFORD, WESTWARD HO! and APPLEDORE RAILWAY.

OPENING OF NEW HALTE AT CORNBOROUGH.

(For Abbotsham Cliffs).

YESTERDAY, Whit-Monday, May 31st, 1909, a New Halte was Opened at Cornborough (for Abbotsham Cliffs), at which

TRAINS WILL STOP

To pick up or set down Passengers

DAILY

During daylight.
Fares same as to and from Abbotsham Road.

Passengers wishing to alight at this Halte must inform the Conductor on joining the Train.

HENRY SOWDEN, General Manager.

apparently popular with walkers who could start or end their exertions at this point.

In August 1909, the Company had applied to the Board of Trade for extension of time for "completing the railway and making a new loop near the School of Art corner". The Bideford Council had formally objected, but the Board of Trade had advised they did not feel justified in refusing the extension. The following week – 17th August – a petition was received by the Council from residents on the Quay requesting an approach to the Railway Company: "to take some means to prevent the loud and continuous nuisance produced by engines when standing on the Quay. The continual clatter was a great annoyance and inconvenience to all living in the vicinity." A letter was sent to the Company. A month later it was reported that Henry Sowden of the Company had replied that he had issued instructions to drivers that they must do all they possibly could to avoid this and sincerely trusted that there would be no further cause for complaint. He also mentioned some required attention to the wood blocks on the Quay, and suggested this be left until "after the visitors had gone". The Council agreed!

Under the 1905 Light Railway Order provision was made for a loop line on the Pill (mentioned briefly earlier) – Railway Number 4 – but this was never built, and on 25th September 1909 application was made for the abandonment of this line.

THE BIDEFORD, WESTWARD HO! & APPLEDORE RAILWAY

A Journey Down the Line

The passenger wishing to make the journey from Bideford to Appledore would, after purchasing a ticket from the Company's office on the Quay, make his way to the train, which would be standing on the track adjacent to the promenade. The loop in the centre of the roadway was generally only used by engines to run round their trains. The track here was of the "tramway" type, level with the roadway and set into wooden blocks.

Starting off down the Quay, the line curved gently right, over the point for the wharf siding, which was operated from a small ground frame, and then turned sharply left, the tracks passing the Art School on the left and the then recently erected statue of Charles Kingsley to the right. The line now ran over the reclaimed land known as **The Pill or Curtis's Marsh**. The line became railway proper here, with fully ballasted sleeper laid track. Passing the Park, the line turned again to the right where a stop was made at **Strand Road Halt**. There were no facilities here, but the spot became a well used request stop.

The line then straightened and ran up towards **Bideford Yard** where the carriage and locomotive sheds were situated. A 6 chain long passing loop here was controlled by a small signal box fitted with 14 levers: 11 in use and 3 spare. The two road carriage shed ran off the loop, whereas the engine shed – also with two roads – ran off the main line, after the loop. Both access points were facing trains travelling in the down direction towards Appledore. The Yard was protected by signals in both directions. Other facilities included a coal store for loco coal, a small office and staff mess room.

Curving round to the left, the line then crossed the level crossing over **Chanter's Lane** with its crossing keeper's cottage.

Only 300 yards further round the bend, **Causeway Crossing** was reached with its tall signal box and single platform. The box operated the signals that controlled the gates and the crossing both here and the previous one at Chanter's Lane. A cottage was built here for the crossing keeper. The railway then ran in an almost straight line up the pleasant Kenwith Valley with open fields to the left and gently wooded areas to the right.

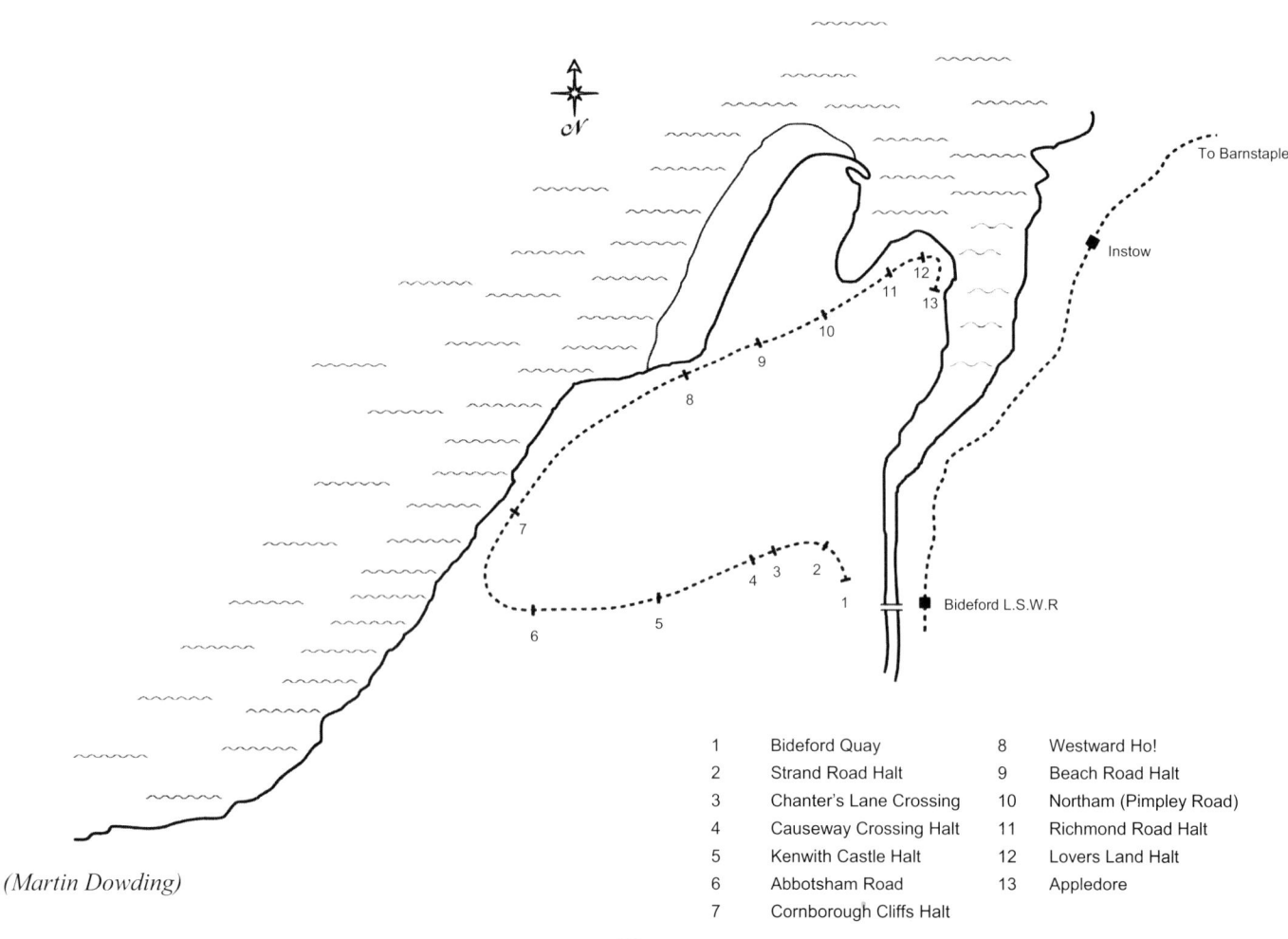

(Martin Dowding)

1	Bideford Quay	8	Westward Ho!
2	Strand Road Halt	9	Beach Road Halt
3	Chanter's Lane Crossing	10	Northam (Pimpley Road)
4	Causeway Crossing Halt	11	Richmond Road Halt
5	Kenwith Castle Halt	12	Lovers Land Halt
6	Abbotsham Road	13	Appledore
7	Cornborough Cliffs Halt		

OPERATION AND EXTENSION

Locomotive and train near Strand Road Halt.
(Bideford Library)

A delightful view of locomotive number 2 "Kingsley" on the Pill near Strand Road Halt with a single coach train. The driver appears to be in the shadows on the footplate, with the fireman sitting on the left hand toolbox and the guard or conductor on the front steps of the coach. Another employee or passenger poses on the rear steps.
(Chris Leigh Collection)

Another scene on the Pill with the bandstand to the left of the front engine. The two engines are "Kingsley" and "Grenville". On the train engine, the fireman on the front of the footplate is probably about to alight having been on watch whilst the train left the Quay. The presence of the second locomotive in the background is interesting. Perhaps this one brought the train in and ran out coupled to the rear of the train as far as this. After the train has left, it will probably run light engine back to the shed. The train seems to be well patronised.
(Roger Griffiths Collection)

THE BIDEFORD, WESTWARD HO! & APPLEDORE RAILWAY

Kenwith Castle Halt was the next stop and here too, a level crossing was provided. It was from here that the Clovelly line would have branched off, had it been built.

The gradient then increased as the line climbed to the half way point at **Abbotsham Road**. A passing loop here was provided with platforms on each side and an 8-lever signal box controlled the crossing and signals. Wilder country was then encountered as the climb continued through deep cuttings and as these were cleared, spectacular views of the rugged coast burst into sight as the line turned sharply right.

Cornborough Cliffs Halte was perched on top of the cliffs exposed to the wild Atlantic weather. The single platform here opened in 1909 and proved to be a popular stop

Above: A mixed train bound for Westward Ho! near Cornborough with the brake van attached behind the two coaches.
(Bideford Library)

Left: "Torridge" heads a Bideford train out from the little windswept Halt on Cornborough Cliffs.
(Rob Dark Collection)

74

OPERATION AND EXTENSION

A view from the edge of Cornborough Cliffs showing the railway winding its way towards what little then existed of Westward Ho!. Seafield House and Merley House are in the centre of the picture. (Tom Bartlett Postcard Collection)

There seems no shortage of passengers on the "up" platform as two trains pass at Westward Ho! (Chris Leigh Collection)

THE BIDEFORD, WESTWARD HO! & APPLEDORE RAILWAY

for walkers wishing to start or finish their walk along the coast.

The line then descended along the cliff tops, running downhill past Seafield House, the Grand Nassau Baths and the Bath Hotel before **Westward Ho!** station with its twin platforms and tidy buildings was reached. **Westward Ho!** was the centre of the railway in terms of facilities for, as well as the twin 320ft long platforms, there were level crossings at each end of the platforms, an 8-lever signal box, and a 2-lever ground frame controlling the signals and crossings. Waiting rooms, toilet facilities, a refreshment room and bookstall were all to be found here. The most impressive building was the Station Hall, which the Company provided for entertainments and concerts. This was designed to attract local and tourist patronage particularly during the summer months and was fully licensed for music, dancing and the sale of alcohol!

Leaving Westward Ho! the train passed the **Gas Works** with its single siding running off to the right. A small ground frame controlled this siding, which was for the delivery of coal for use in the Works.

Crossing **Avon Lane** and the request Halt at **Beach Road**, the line continued, passing the Royal North Devon Golf Club on the left with sweeping views out over the Burrows to the sea.

Northam station, boasting a platform and waiting room, was once the terminus, but the loop line and signal box were removed when the extension to Appledore was opened. Another level crossing here was then passed and the next stop as the train headed north-east was at **Richmond Road**. A further level crossing and short platform with a small shelter for passengers was provided here.

Curving round to the right, the line passed Lover's Lane Halt with its shelter-less platform and then quickly ran in to the smart terminus at **Appledore**. A run-round loop had a low 300 foot platform on the down side, which was provided with waiting rooms, booking facilities and toilets. A 10-lever signal box was also built on the platform. A footbridge spanned the line at the entry to the loop line and a short siding ran off the right-hand side of the loop. Locomotives were catered for by an engine shed with coal and water facilities, the latter by way of a water crane being provided in the shed. It was usual for an engine to be stabled here overnight to haul the first train of the day. Two cottages were also built adjacent to the site for the use of the Company's employees.

A busy scene at Westward Ho! with plenty of passengers awaiting the next train. The level crossing gates are closed to allow road traffic to cross. (Chris Leigh Collection)

OPERATION AND EXTENSION

A train in the platform at Westward Ho! The locomotive is probably "Torridge". Another train departs in the opposite direction. (Lens of Sutton)

The waiting room at Westward Ho! with a train just arrived from Bideford. The carriage steps are prominent in this view. (Marilyn Hughes, Westward Ho! History Group)

THE BIDEFORD, WESTWARD HO! & APPLEDORE RAILWAY

The troop of minstrels that regularly entertained at the Station Hall at Westward Ho! (Beaford Archive)

A view of the Station Hall at Westward Ho! showing the elegant interior. This is probably after the railway closed when the Hall was used as a café. (Marilyn Hughes, Westward Ho! History Group)

OPERATION AND EXTENSION

A rear view of the Station Hall showing the platform fencing behind it. The benches in the grounds were rescued from the ill-fated Westward Ho! pier. (Marilyn Hughes, Westward Ho! History Group)

An interesting view of Appledore station, with Mr Moody the stationmaster overseeing matters. The locomotive appears to be taking water from the elevated tank to the right of the picture. It will then set back to run round its train. (Lens of Sutton)

THE HUNSLET ENGINE CO. LTD *Engineers* LEEDS ENGLAND

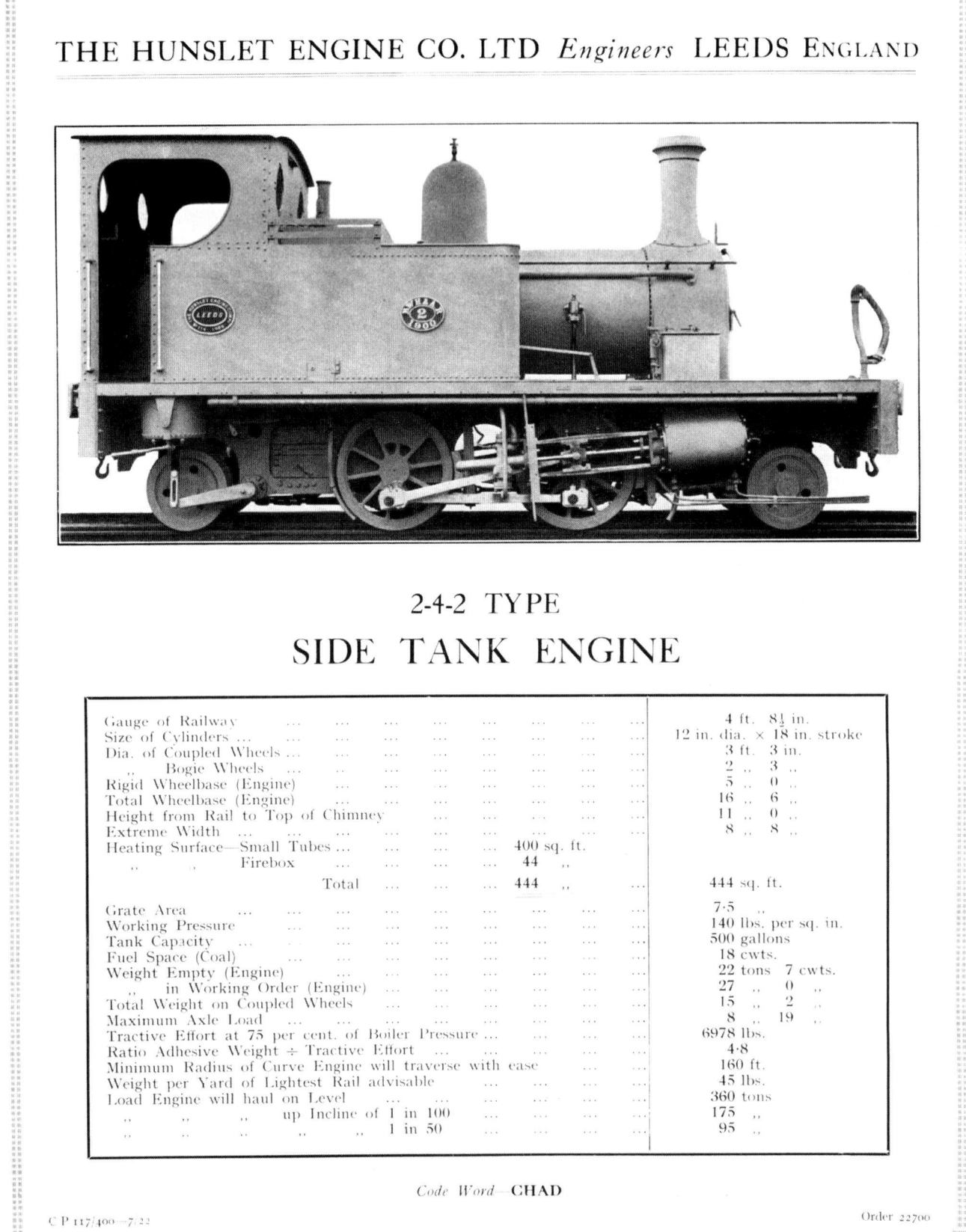

2-4-2 TYPE
SIDE TANK ENGINE

Gauge of Railway	4 ft. 8½ in.
Size of Cylinders	12 in. dia. × 18 in. stroke
Dia. of Coupled Wheels	3 ft. 3 in.
" Bogie Wheels	2 " 3 "
Rigid Wheelbase (Engine)	5 " 0 "
Total Wheelbase (Engine)	16 " 6 "
Height from Rail to Top of Chimney	11 " 0 "
Extreme Width	8 " 8 "
Heating Surface—Small Tubes	400 sq. ft.
" " Firebox	44 "
Total	444 sq. ft.
Grate Area	7·5
Working Pressure	140 lbs. per sq. in.
Tank Capacity	500 gallons
Fuel Space (Coal)	18 cwts.
Weight Empty (Engine)	22 tons 7 cwts.
" in Working Order (Engine)	27 " 0 "
Total Weight on Coupled Wheels	15 " 2 "
Maximum Axle Load	8 " 19 "
Tractive Effort at 75 per cent. of Boiler Pressure	6978 lbs.
Ratio Adhesive Weight ÷ Tractive Effort	4·8
Minimum Radius of Curve Engine will traverse with ease	160 ft.
Weight per Yard of Lightest Rail advisable	45 lbs.
Load Engine will haul on Level	360 tons
" " " " up Incline of 1 in 100	175 "
" " " " 1 in 50	95 "

Code Word— **CHAD**

C P 117/400—7/22   Order 22700

Chapter 5

Rolling Stock and Infrastructure

Locomotives

The Hunslet Engine Company of Leeds was favoured with the order for the motive power for the line, and this order is noted in Hunslet's records as being for three locomotive engines of "four-wheeled coupled double-bogie type". The order was apparently placed by the then contractor, Charles Chadwell. Utilising certain standard parts from the Hunslet range, such as cylinders and other mechanical parts and having the unmistakable Hunslet cab and chimney profiles, three engines of the 2-4-2T configuration were built at the Company's works in Leeds in 1900, being delivered early in 1901.

The engines were fitted with side tanks, having a capacity of 500 gallons of water, and outside cylinders of 12in bore and 18in stroke driving the rear coupled axle. Driving wheels were 3ft 3in diameter with a 5ft wheelbase, and front and trailing wheels were 2ft 3in diameter. Provision for carrying up to 18 cwt of coal was made, apparently on top of the rear part of the water tanks, although photographs do not seem to show much of this – possibly a bag or two was squeezed in on the footplate! The engines were fitted with vacuum brakes and, with a total heating surface of 444 sq ft and a working boiler pressure of 140psi, these sturdy looking little engines weighed in at 27 tons.

Opposite page: The manufacturer's catalogue page of their 2-4-2 type locomotive, as supplied to the Company. This includes the manufacturer's official photograph of Hunslet works number 714, BWHAR number 2 "Kingsley". The works and owners plates, motion and sand pipes and clearly seen.

Above: An official picture of number 2 again, this time after the fitting of the protective skirts. (Chris Leigh Collection)

THE BIDEFORD, WESTWARD HO! & APPLEDORE RAILWAY

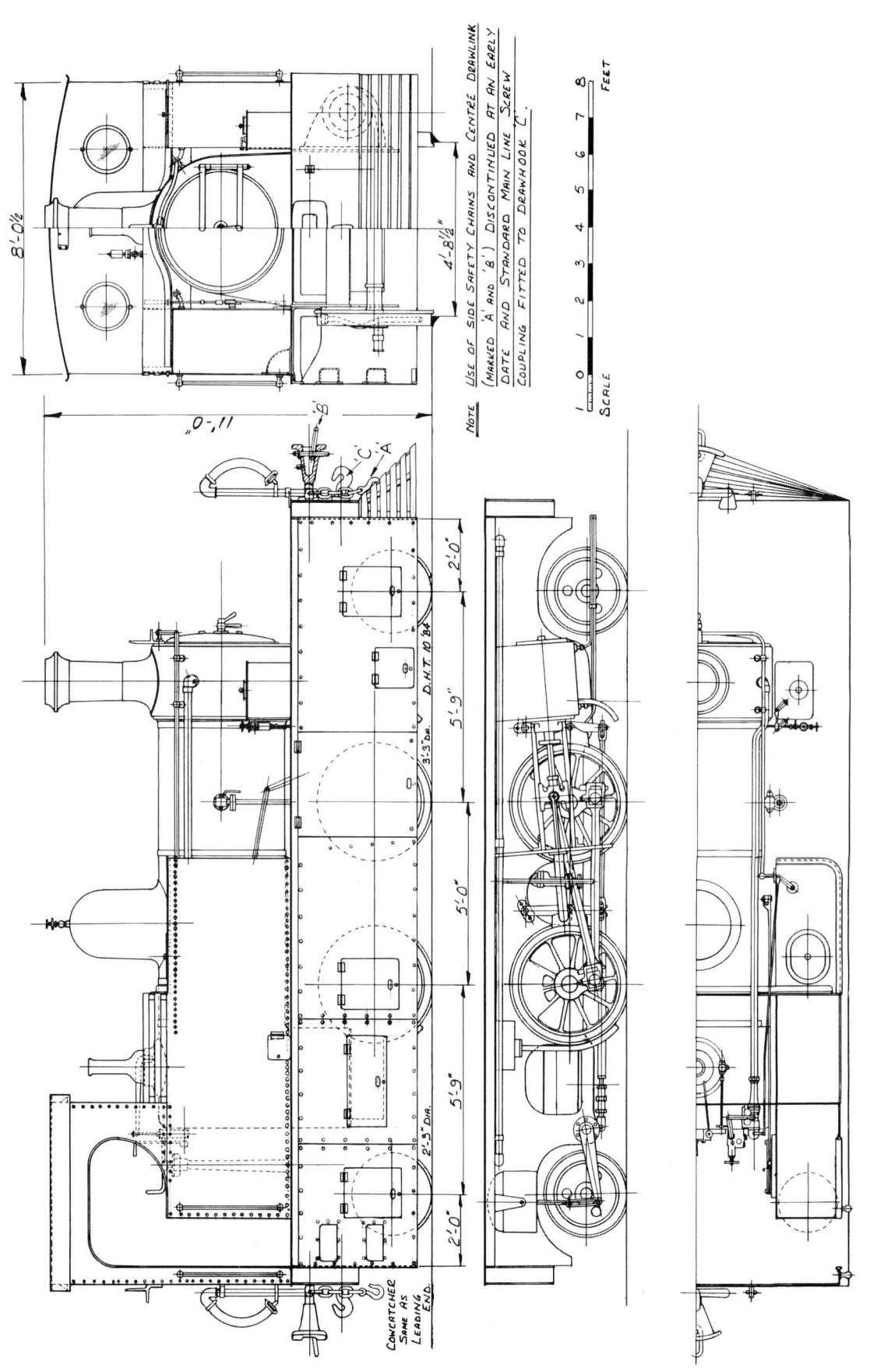

Donald Townsley's drawing of the locomotives, taken from the original drawings.

ROLLING STOCK AND INFRASTRUCTURE

A superb close up of "Kingsley". The details of the lining can be clearly seen and the owner's number is also visible on the cabside plate. A pile of coal is also apparent on top of the side tank just under the left hand spectacle glass. The central buffer, side chains and vacuum brake hose are also clear to see. The bolts that would have held the conventional buffers on to the buffer beam are also apparent. Notice also the hinged flaps in the side sheets to allow access to the working parts. (Bath Photographic, Bideford)

83

THE BIDEFORD, WESTWARD HO! & APPLEDORE RAILWAY

"Kingsley" at Appledore showing off her "cowcatcher". Note that she carries her name on the tank side, between the maker's and owner's plates. The name is presumably painted on and it seems that these names were later removed or covered over as they do not often appear in photographs. The footbridge that spanned the station can just be seen in the background. (Chris Leigh Collection)

The engines had an interesting design of pony truck incorporating a central semi-spherical centre bearing to cater for transverse vertical movement, with a swing link arrangement to provide the side play. The manufacturer's full dimensions and performance figures are as shown in the accompanying table. Don Townsley's lovely drawing of the locomotives is also taken from the Company's records and shows the engines as new, but with the cowcatchers that were fitted soon after they entered service. The vacuum pipe was later lowered to a point below the drawgear.

The Company named the engines *Grenville*, *Kingsley* and *Torridge* and they were numbered 1 (works number 713), 2 (714), and 3 (715) respectively. Each locomotive carried an oval brass maker's plate and a slightly smaller plate bearing the letters BWH&AR with the running number and date of manufacture. As the railway had no turntable, the locomotives spent their relatively short lives always facing the way they were delivered. *Torridge* faced Bideford, whilst *Grenville* and *Kingsley* faced Appledore.

The question of livery has long been a matter for discussion, and photographic evidence as to the livery carried by the trio of engines is difficult to interpret. It has been suggested that the overall colour changed from an original black, through green, cherry red to black again. Lining of off-white or yellow to the side tanks, cab sides, cab rear and wheel skirting has been suggested and lining is clearly visible on some existing photographs. The dome and safety valve cover do seem to have been of polished brass finish. Access to the manufacturer's records now suggests that the engines were turned out in green. The Hunslet painting book states:

"Painted like GNR engines dark green style 4in wide picked out black 1¾ in wide edged strong white line each side. Screen plates like panels, light green. Frames and wheels plain black, inside cab stone colour lined black and white, inside frames and buffer beams vermillion."

This description matches that given for Great Northern Railway locomotives in Ernest F. Carter's book *Britain's Railway Liveries*. This would therefore support the idea that the engines were in fact painted green – but two shades of green – light green with dark green panels lined out in black edged in white. Photographic evidence supports the black and white lining idea, but whether two shades of green were used is virtually impossible to determine.

ROLLING STOCK AND INFRASTRUCTURE

Technical details of the Hunslet locomotives			
Gauge	4ft 8½in	Tank capacity	500 gallons
Cylinders	12in diameter x 18in stroke	Fuel space (coal)	18cwt
Diameter of coupled wheels	3ft 3in	Engine weight empty	22 ton 7cwt
Diameter of bogie wheels	2ft 3in	Engine weight in working order	27 ton 0cwt
Rigid wheelbase: engine	5ft 0in	Total weight of coupled wheels	15 ton 2cwt
Total wheelbase: engine	16ft 6in	Maximum axle load	8 ton 19cwt
Height: rail to top of chimney	11ft 0in	Tractive effort at 75% of boiler pressure	6,978lb
Extreme width	8ft 8in	Ratio of adhesive weight to tractive effort	4.8
Heating surfaces:		Maximum radius of curve engine will traverse with ease	160ft
Small tubes: 400 sq ft		Weight per yard of lightest rail advisable	45lb
Firebox: 44 sq ft	Total: 444 sq ft	Load engine will haul on level	360 tons
Grate area	7.5 sq ft	Load engine will haul up incline of 1 in 100	175 tons
Working pressure	140psi	Load engine will haul up incline of 1 in 50	95 tons

A good close up view of the locomotive heading the official opening train. This shot shows much detail of the lining applied to the engine, the buffing gear and chains, and the tool boxes on the front of the footplate. Note also the swivelling front and rear spectacle glasses.
(Marilyn Hughes, Westward Ho! History Group)

THE BIDEFORD, WESTWARD HO! & APPLEDORE RAILWAY

Locomotive number 1 or 2 simmers quietly on the Quay, looking a little weary. Part of the side plating has been removed for easier access to the motion. (Chris Leigh Collection)

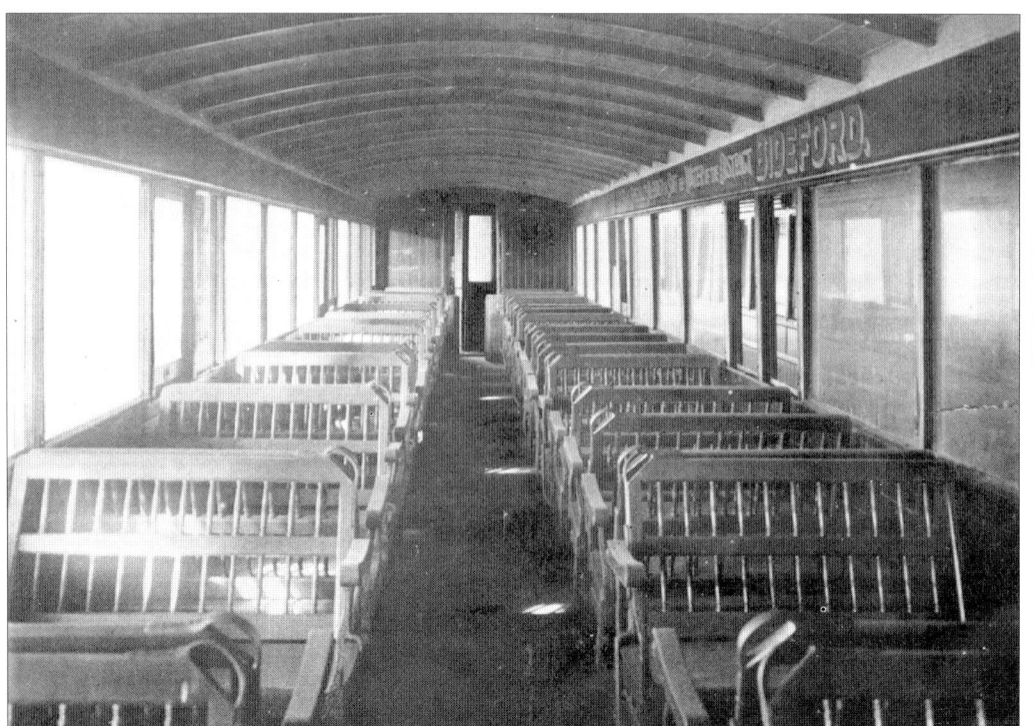

Above: One of the wooden ventilator knobs from inside one of the coaches

Left: An interior view of one of the third class coaches. (Chris Leigh Collection)

ROLLING STOCK AND INFRASTRUCTURE

Coaching stock

The carriages were supplied by the Bristol Carriage & Wagon Company to an elaborate American style and eventually numbered six in total. The first to arrive in Bideford were 4 cars, of which 3 had seating for 10 first class and 40 (some reports state only 32) third class passengers. The fourth car had seating for 30 third class passengers with a guard's/baggage compartment. The coaches measured some 48ft long and 9ft wide extending to 11ft 3in over the steps. Each carriage was carried on two four-wheel bogies with 3ft 1in diameter wheels placed at 6ft centres.

A central corridor ran through each car and the seats were of the reversible "tramcar" type. The carriages were clad in polished teak, with interiors panelled in polished oak. The ceilings were painted in pale green, picked out in gold, with dark green mouldings, and they were lit by acetylene gas. Double-faced clocks were installed centrally at least in some of the cars.

The exact date when the remaining two cars were delivered is uncertain, but from details given in the local newspapers, it would seem that they may well have arrived in time for the opening of the extension to Appledore – maybe late in 1907 or early 1908. It has been stated that they were built locally, but this cannot be confirmed. However, as they were of similar design, layout and construction to the first batch, it would seem unlikely that they were made locally. This second pair was third class only, 66ft long and 9ft wide over the bodywork. They had seating for 84 passengers.

The cars were well upholstered with American leather in the first class and "rep" (a corded textile fabric) in the third class. The Company name was emblazoned along the outside of each carriage and in the centre was a wooden replica of the Bideford coat of arms. The cars were fitted with a centre buffer and coupling.

(Clive Fairchild Collection)

A close up of the first class end of a composite coach. Note the American veranda style entrance, the wood panelling and large steps. (Chris Leigh Collection)

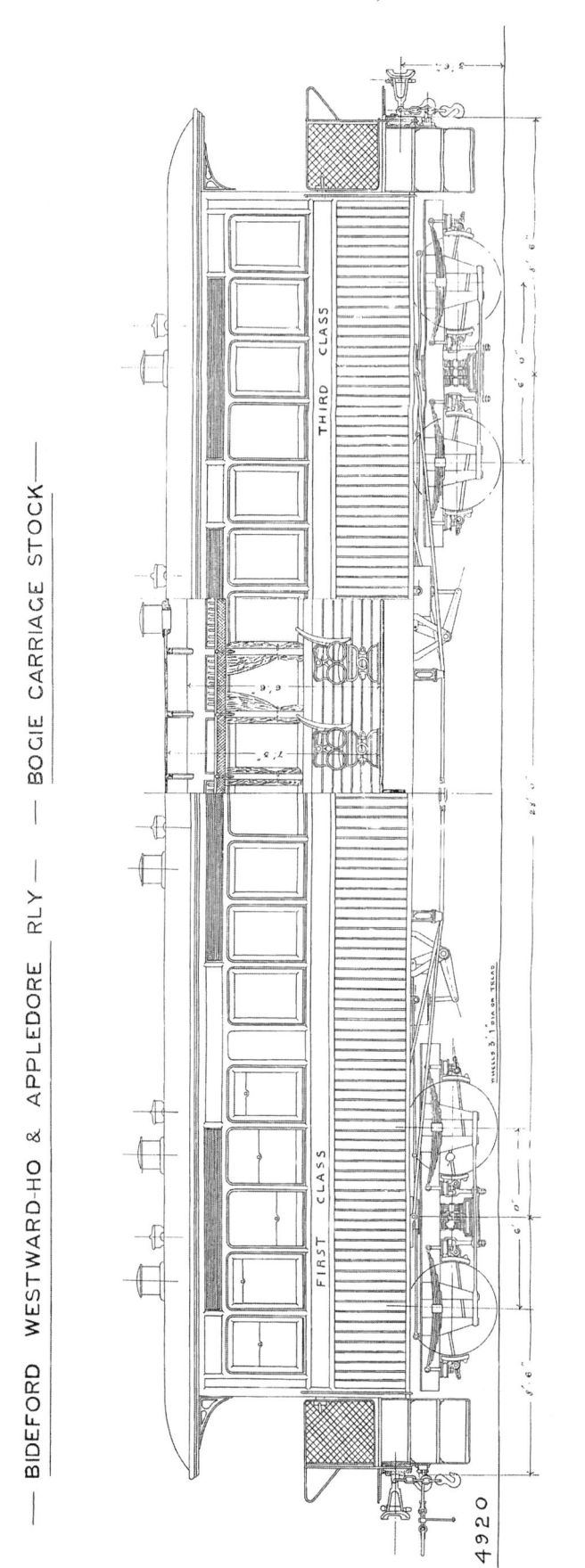

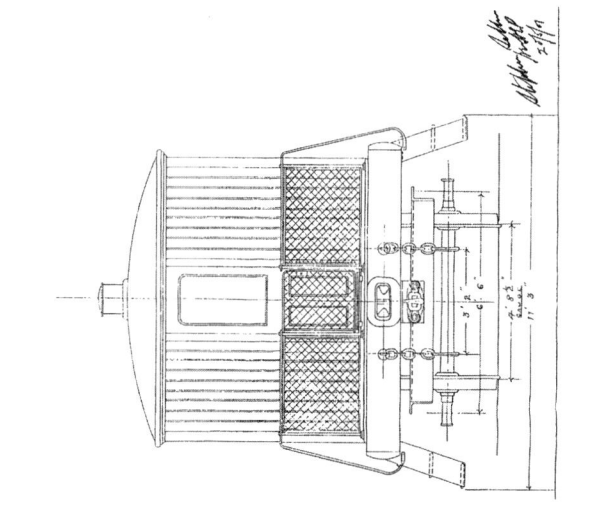

THE BIDEFORD, WESTWARD HO! & APPLEDORE RAILWAY

— BIDEFORD WESTWARD-HO & APPLEDORE RLY — BOGIE CARRIAGE STOCK —

Above and left: Part of the railway company's drawings for the composite coaches.

Right: An interior view of one of the composite coaches. (Felton Vowler)

ROLLING STOCK AND INFRASTRUCTURE

The manufacturer's official photograph of one of the composite coaches. (Roger Carpenter)

Goods wagons

Goods stock was quite small in number, and it is not totally clear how many vehicles were owned. Some reports suggest six open wagons, four vans and a brake van, but this does not seem to be substantiated. Others give eight open wagons and a brake van cum goods van, a total of nine vehicles. However, the article in the *B.E.T. Monthly Gazette* clearly states that there were 6 open wagons, 2 covered goods wagons and a box van, so we must assume that the owners of the company were correct. The open wagons would have been used to carry coal from Bideford Quay to Westward Ho! Gas Works as well as for the Company's own service requirements carrying permanent way materials, stores, etc.

The maker is unknown and details of the stock are difficult to establish, although the "opens" seem to have been 4 plank wagons with the BWH&AR lettering on the sides. Livery can only be guessed at, but was probably the ubiquitous mid grey. The wagons were fitted with a centre buffer and coupling, and possibly also chains.

A poor quality, but rare, view of the goods/brake van at the end of the Appledore siding. The unique single buffer stop can be clearly seen. (Clive Fairchild Collection)

89

THE BIDEFORD, WESTWARD HO! & APPLEDORE RAILWAY

Signalling

Little detail has been discovered as to the installation of the signalling system although most accounts credit the firm of Saxby & Farmer with the work. A drawing of Appledore station dated 1908 showing the signalling layout bears the name of the firm of F.A. Atkinson & Co., Railway Signal Engineers, London, but no further details have been discovered.

The line was worked by means of train staff and tickets combined with the absolute block system using telephone communication between signal boxes instead of block instruments. In simplistic terms this system splits the railway into block sections and a train is not allowed into any section without possession of the staff, basically a short stick carrying the name of the section to which it applies – for example, Abbotsham Road to Westward Ho!

The staff was handed to the driver of the train by the signalman at the start of the section – in the case mentioned, at Abbotsham Road – and was handed over to the signalman at Westward Ho! on arrival. The next train back to Abbotsham Road took the staff back, thus ensuring only one train was in the section at a time.

In the event that another train was timetabled to run over the same section before a return journey was made, use was made of the ticket part of the system. In this case, prior to the first train leaving, the driver was shown the staff but this was kept at the signal box. The driver was instead given a paper ticket with details of the section to which it applied printed on it and this was his authority to proceed. However, before the signalman authorised any movement, he had to telephone the signalman at the next block post – Westward Ho! in this illustration – to confirm that the line was clear.

The first train then proceeded with the paper ticket and the following train could proceed with the actual staff, once the signalman had confirmed with his colleague at the next box that the line was again clear. In practice, it is doubtful if the traffic on the line was intensive enough to warrant the use of tickets very often, but the system was flexible enough to cater for this eventuality.

The Bideford, Westward Ho! & Appledore was originally split into three block sections: Bideford Yard to Mudcott (renamed Abbotsham Road once the platforms were installed), Mudcott to Westward Ho!, and Westward Ho! to Northam. Once the line along the Quay was opened, a new section was added as Bideford Quay to Bideford Yard. When the extension to Appledore was opened, the section from Westward Ho! to Northam was extended through to Appledore, thus maintaining four block sections.

Details of the actual signals themselves are scarce; generally home or stop signals were used to protect crossings and stations. It is thought that the only use of distant, or warning, signals was at Chanters Lane and Causeway Crossings and Appledore station. Colonel Yorke had insisted upon each of the two adjacent crossings having its own set of signals and as they were so close together, a warning distant was erected at each to indicate the state of the home signal at the next crossing. At Appledore, Major Pringle had made a requirement for a distant signal on the approach to the station as there was insufficient distance for sighting of the home signal.

Unused Train Staff Ticket number 115 for the section from Westward Ho! to Northam. This is an example of the ticket which would have been issued to the engine driver for a single line section, where the staff could not be released as a further train was to follow.
(Maureen Richards, Westward Ho! History Group)

ROLLING STOCK AND INFRASTRUCTURE

Right: A nice view of Abbotsham Road station. Note the signal wire and point rodding on the right of the picture (Rob Dark Collection)

Below: A good view of the miniature home/starter signal at the end of the Abbotsham Road platform. The home signal on the other side of the line can also be seen. Point rodding and a signal wire are visible on the right of the picture. Note the low platforms and minimal Facilities.
(Roger Griffiths Collection)

THE BIDEFORD, WESTWARD HO! & APPLEDORE RAILWAY

Causeway Crossing signal box. The box towers over the cottage and commands the clear views demanded by Colonel Yorke. The level crossing gates are closed against the horse drawn traffic awaiting the departure of the train. The chap in the foreground bears a striking resemblance to the chap on the right of the group laying the point work on the Quay in the photograph on page 23. (Chris Leigh Collection)

A down train heads off from Causeway Crossing into the open country towards Kenwith Castle Halt. The signal post with two arms can be clearly seen. These were the home signal for the crossing and the distant for the crossing at Chanters Lane, just round the corner. (Ian Pope Collection)

ROLLING STOCK AND INFRASTRUCTURE

Westward Ho! station in all its glory, with the platform mounted signal box on the left. Point rodding can be seen running under the tracks and towards the camera. (Marilyn Hughes, Westward Ho! History Group)

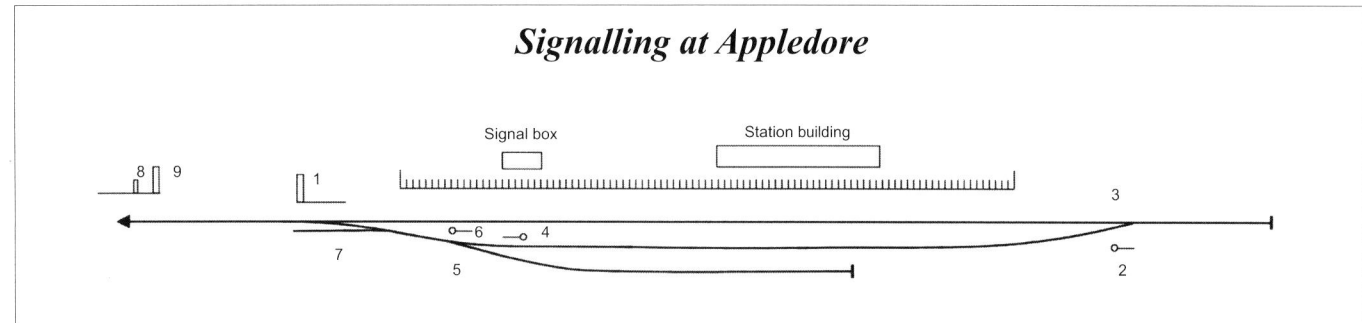

Signalling at Appledore

Appledore station signalling plan based upon the original proposal with details of the signal lever allocation. (Martin Dowding)

The signalling at Appledore was controlled from a small platform-mounted signal box. The Board of Trade inspection report makes reference to there being ground signals, "a home and starting signal" as well as a distant signal on the approach to the station. The plan indicates a starter and, in the up direction, a home and what was probably a shunt signal on one arm outside the station. The distant signal is not shown. As the requirement for this was not envisaged until the official inspection, it was presumably then added and took up the spare lever in the box.

The lever allocation in the signal box was as follows:

1. Up starter signal
2. Ground signal for run-round loop entry up points
3. Up points for end of run-round loop
4. Ground signal for siding entry points
5. Siding entry points
6. Ground signal for run-round loop up exit points
7. Down facing points (including interlocked trap point) at end of run-round loop
8. Down shunt signal arm
9. Down main home signal
10. Spare (later, down distant signal)

THE BIDEFORD, WESTWARD HO! & APPLEDORE RAILWAY

Civil engineering works

There was some heavy construction work on the first part of the line with cuttings up to 32ft deep needed, and embankments rising up to 22ft. Two underbridges were needed with spans of 10ft and 12ft, constructed of steel troughs on masonry abutments. Five culverts of similar construction were also provided.

The extension line was of much easier construction, with no cutting or embankment exceeding 7ft. The only bridge was the footbridge at the entrance to Appledore station.

A view of an underbridge near Westward Ho!, taken after the line had closed. This shows the high standard of construction used throughout the railway. (Chris Leigh Collection)

Track

The original line from Bideford to Westward Ho! was laid with steel flat bottomed rail weighing 60 lb per yard. This was fastened to sleepers of 9ft x 9in x 4½in by fang bolts, clips and dog spikes. Ballast was of broken stone to a depth of approximately 12in below the sleepers. The rails were fastened with 16in long fishplates bolted by means of ⅞in diameter bolts secured by 1½in square nuts. An interesting note on the official drawing states that half of the fishplates were to have round holes and half to have square holes. The holes in the rail were to be round.

The track originally laid up the middle of the Quay had a groove that was between 1¾ and 2in wide, which Colonel Yorke in his initial inspection condemned as being too wide. The groove was actually made by bolting a piece of steel strip alongside the rail, separated from it by a wooden block. The resultant gap was considered dangerous and a new method of construction was introduced using a shaped piece of steel bolted directly to the rail at the closer spacing of $1^{5}/_{16}$in demanded by Colonel Yorke.

It would seem that a cheaper source of rail had been found for the extension to Appledore as this was laid with double headed second-hand steel rails originally weighing 80lb per yard. The track in Appledore station itself and at the start of the new section however, was laid with 60lb rail. The sleepers – also second-hand – were some ½in deeper at 5in and ballast was apparently laid to 15in under these.

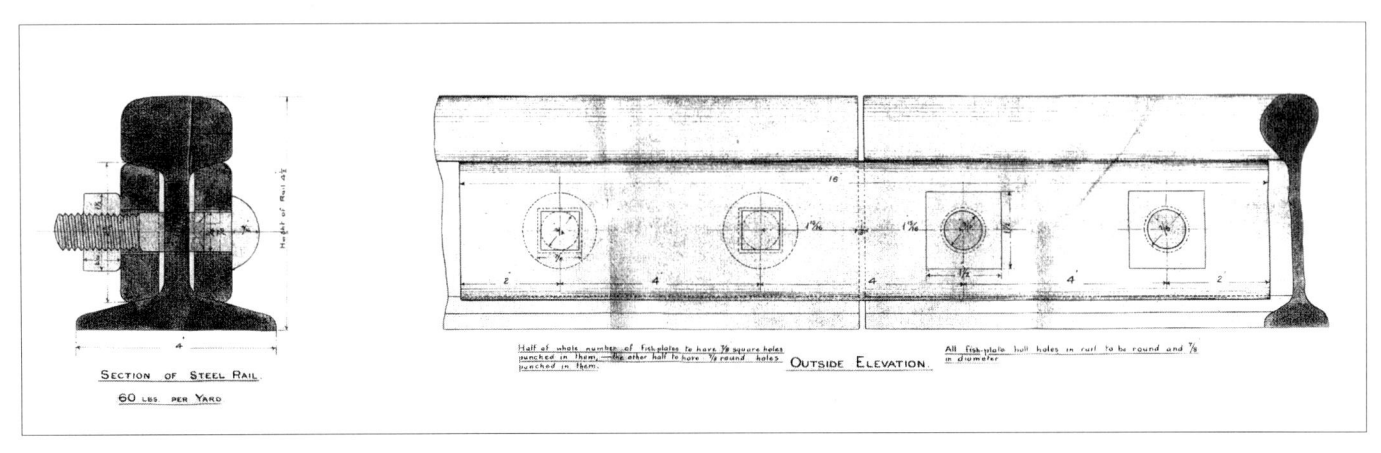

The official drawings of rail and fishplates for the line.

Chapter 6

The Final Years

Traffic, Timetables and Fares

With the railway now operational throughout its length, it is perhaps pertinent to consider the traffic of the line vis-à-vis the timing of trains and the fare structure.

A glance at the timetables for autumn 1902 to spring 1903 shows eleven trains scheduled in both up and down directions during the week, with the addition of three on Sundays (except in the winter). The first train was scheduled to leave Bideford at 9.34am and this train formed the first departure from Northam at 9.55am. Subsequent departures were within three or four minutes of arrival at both ends of the line. It was not until after arriving back at Bideford at 1.37pm that a 23 minute break gave time for either a change of locomotive or stock, or for coaling and watering of the first engine. Thereafter the rest of the day's service could have still been handled by one engine without much effort. The last two trains of the day – one to Westward Ho! and back only – were advertised as Tuesdays and Saturdays only, to cater for local Market Days.

The summer 1903 timetable shows a service increased to sixteen up and down trains per weekday, with four each way on Sundays. The last train of the day on Wednesdays and Saturdays left Bideford at 9.25pm for Westward Ho! only, as opposed to 9.00pm the rest of the week. The return was at 9.45pm instead of 9.18pm. The first train of the day still did

A view up Station Road toward Westward Ho! station some years later than the view on page 53. The properties on the left have been newly built and tourists appear to be flocking in to the town. The relatively large number of motor vehicles and holiday-makers is a portent of things to come! (Tom Bartlett Postcard Collection)

THE BIDEFORD, WESTWARD HO! & APPLEDORE RAILWAY

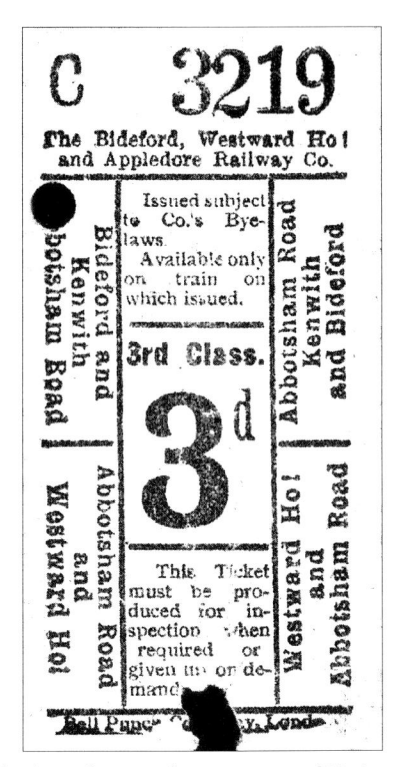

Left: A third class ticket issued from Richmond Road to Northam, or Northam to Beach Road. (Marilyn Hughes, Westward Ho! History Group)
Centre: A third class 2½d ticket from Appledore to Beach Road. (Ian Pringle Collection)
Right: A third class 3d ticket from Bideford to Kenwith/Abbotsham Road. (Ian Pringle Collection)

not manage to leave before 9.34am. A total of six trains terminated at Westward Ho! rather than Northam – three in the mid-afternoon and three alternate ones later in the day. With a much increased service, the need for two trains was obvious and from a close study of the timetable, it would appear that the first train operated the 9.34, 10.40 and 11.25 services from Bideford with the second train taking the 11.57am out, crossing the returning 11.25 (now the 11.46 from Northam) at Abbotsham Road. The first locomotive then had a leisurely two hours or more to coal and water before taking charge of the 2.25pm. Both locomotives were seemingly then employed for the rest of the day, with a break for one in the late afternoon or early evening.

The summer timetable for the following year also shows a service of sixteen up and down working during the week, with four each way on Sundays. A 9.34am departure was still listed as the first train of the day. Northam was not served by the last three services of the day, the latest time for catching a train from there being 7.15pm. Two trains were of course still required. The first train operated the 9.34, 10.40 and 11.30 services from Bideford with the second train taking the 11.50am out, crossing the returning 11.30 (now the 11.50 from Northam) at Abbotsham Road. The first locomotive then had a couple of hours to coal and water before leaving with the 2.20pm service. Both locomotives were then employed for the rest of the day, with a break for one in the

early evening when one took the 5.45pm and 6.40pm trains out and back to Northam, with the other rounding off the day with the 7.45pm and 9.10pm trains to Westward Ho! and back.

Moving on to 1908, when the line was fully operational to Appledore, we see twelve return journeys timetabled for May that year with three trains on Sundays. An earlier start of 7.50am for the first train of the day is noted. The last train of the day however, the 9.20pm to Appledore and back, was a Tuesday and Saturday only Market Day special. Quite how the service was operated from a locomotive point of view is unclear; the timing of the services would have allowed for operation by one engine, apart from the very tight turn-round times which generally were only a few minutes. These would not have given enough time for coaling and watering and it is assumed that a second train was brought into operation in the middle of the day.

The published timetable for March and April of 1912 (reproduced on the opposite page) shows a much reduced service of only five up and down workings during the week, with two at weekends from 5th May. The first train of the day was from Appledore at 8.25am which arrived at Bideford at 8.55am but did not set off on its return until 10.00am. Having reached Appledore at 10.30am this train then scuttled back to Bideford five minutes later where it rested from

THE FINAL YEARS

11.05am until returning to Appledore at 1.00pm. Sporadic is the word that comes to mind when looking at this timetable! An interesting feature of this 1912 timetable is that it lists all the stations and halts on the line – Bideford Quay, Strand Road*, The Lane*, Causeway*, Kenwith Castle*, Abbotsham Road, Cornborough*, Westward Ho!, Beach Road*, Northam, Richmond Road*, Lover's Lane*, and Appledore. Those stops marked * were noted as being Halts. ("Passengers wishing to alight at any Halt must inform the Conductor on joining the train.")

Over its short life, the railway operated nine or ten trains during the winter and up to about sixteen during the summer months, but the writing seems to have been on the wall in its later years with traffic not warranting such intensive services as had been provided in earlier years. Indications from annual reports suggest that the line was losing money at this stage in its life.

The March – April timetable for 1912.

THE BIDEFORD, WESTWARD HO! & APPLEDORE RAILWAY

PASSENGERS FARES (Including the usual quantity of luggage):	1st class	1st class	3rd class	3rd class
BETWEEN	Single	Return	Single	Return
Bideford and Westward Ho!	8d	1s 0d	4½d	6d
Bideford and Northam	~	~	5d	6d
Bideford and The Lane or Causeway	2d	~	1d	
Bideford and Appledore	10d	1s 3d	6d	8d
Abbotsham Road and Bideford or Northam	6d	10d	3d	
Westward Ho! and Northam	3d	4d	2d	3d

The fare structure on the line seemed to remain unaltered during its life and the table above shows the fares published after the opening of the extension to Appledore, the only alteration being the inclusion of the new section

Tickets were generally issued by conductors on the trains, although booking office facilities were to be found at Bideford, Westward Ho! and Appledore. The tickets were of the upright tramway type rather than the more popular horizontal format used by most railway companies. Fares, and tickets, for journeys other than as mentioned in the table did exist. For example the third class single fare between Westward Ho! and Appledore was 2½d. In 1912, third class workmen's tickets were sold between Bideford and Northam (5d return) and Bideford and Westward Ho! (6d return). A weekly 1/- ticket covered six single or three return journeys. Market day tickets from Appledore to Bideford were available on Tuesday and Saturdays for 6d return. Parcels were catered for and rates for almost every conceivable type of parcel were available.

One of the most interesting points from the timetables is the late start of the service in the morning. The first train of the day did not leave Bideford until 9.34am, returning from Appledore at 9.55am. This would seem to rule out traffic from manual workers, shop assistants and the like wishing to travel by train to work. When the extension to Appledore was being discussed locally, it was reported that there were some 200 Bideford men employed in the Appledore shipyards and about 60 Appledore girls in the collar factory at Bideford. The shipyard men apparently started work at 6.00am and presumably the collar factory was up and running reasonably early in the day. The developing resort of Westward Ho! with its smart villas and houses no doubt attracted the more affluent professional types who may well have worked in Bideford. It is probable that some of these employed domestic servants who lived in Bideford and thus a two way traffic could well have existed from these sources. Clearly there must have been considerable traffic in people between the three places on a daily basis and one wonders why the Railway Company did not cater for this regular traffic.

The front cover of the official summer 1905 timetable. (Chris Leigh Collection)

THE FINAL YEARS

However, the question of journey length and cost must be considered. Bideford to Appledore was some seven miles by the railway but less than half that by road. Messrs. Dymond & Son of Bideford were well established operators of horse breaks (sic) and ran very comprehensive services between Bideford, Appledore and Westward Ho! Their fares were cheaper than the railway company's and journey times were shorter. Of particular interest to passengers alighting from the LSWR station was a waiting conveyance at the station obviating the need for walking over the bridge to the Bideford, Westward Ho! & Appledore terminus and transfer of luggage. Any connection with the main-line service does not seem to have been of much relevance either. For example the 9.34am from Bideford departed a mere 2 minutes after the up main line train had arrived at the LSWR station over the river. The down LSWR was due at 8.40am which meant a lengthy wait for any prospective passenger.

Interestingly, after the extension to Appledore was opened in 1908, a horse drawn coach was run from Westward Ho! to Clovelly, presumably in the summer months for tourists. Through tickets were available from Instow on the LSWR to cover the ferry over the river, the train from Appledore to Westward Ho! and the coach to Clovelly!

Staff

The *B.E.T. Monthly Gazette* for August 1902 which was discussed earlier, gives a total number of staff as 25 for that date. These staff numbers do not include John Loughlin, the station master at Westward Ho! or his counterpart at Bideford, although it is not clear if the latter had such a post. It is possible that Henry Sowden as Traffic Superintendent, or General Manager as he is also described, may have filled this role.

A total of 5 "drivers, firemen and conductors" tends to suggest that in fact only one train was working at any one time and only one set of crew – driver, fireman and conductor – was required. The extension to Appledore and the need for two trains at some times of the day indicates that additional train crew were then employed, assuming some spare capacity to allow for holidays, sickness, etc. Any staff originally at Northam would no doubt have been moved to Appledore, where Harold Moody became station master. In all probability the total number of staff did not exceed 30. From interviews with a surviving member of staff in the 1960s, Roger Griffiths was able to put names to some of the staff and these are noted below.

- Mr Dicker was employed at the Yard and was either an engineer or a permanent way man.
- Drivers: Messrs F. Palmer, Shephard and Hawkins; all apparently retired LSWR top link drivers.
- Firemen: Messrs Harris (also an engineer), Alfie Curtiss and F. Bucker.
- The signalmen were Mr Spry at Westward Ho! and Mr Furzy at the Causeway.
- Chanters Lane Halt was in the charge of Mr Blackmore.
- Permanent way men were Jack Shears and Ned Kelly.
- The railway company manager was stated as being Mr Henry, although this could be a reference to Henry Sowden, Superintendent and later Manager.

A detachment of the Devon Hussars Yeomanry setting off from Bideford for camp at Westward Ho! The locomotive to the left of the picture is "Torridge" still sporting her name on the tank side. The boy with the hand cart followed behind the horses to sweep up! The shop in the centre background with the awning on the corner is Perkins the fruiterers and florists. The Railway Company office pictured on page 58 is the next one along, away from the camera. (Beaford Archive)

THE BIDEFORD, WESTWARD HO! & APPLEDORE RAILWAY

Twilight

At the half-yearly meeting of the Company on 31st March 1910, the accounts for the half year showed an operating loss of £25 14s 1d; revenue being down due to the bad weather the previous July, August and September. It was agreed to discontinue half-yearly meetings. Captain Molesworth, retiring by rotation was re-elected as a director. These results were clearly a sign of things to come, for it seems that profits were hard to come by from then on and the financial status of the railway must have been very parlous.

In 1913, whilst still apparently happy with their steam locomotives, the Company were investigating the purchase of a petrol railcar for use on the line. In a letter to the Railway Department of the Board of Trade on 25th July 1913, Henry Sowden, the General Manager forwarded copies of two drawings of a railcar "intended to be an improvement on the Cars now in use at Morecambe". The car was to be a 4-wheel double-ended unit with a 10ft wheelbase. Power would be provided by a 60hp Leyland engine. Length overall was to be 31ft 9in with a width of 8ft 7in over fixed steps fitted at each end. Accommodation was to be provided for 32 passengers in 2 rows of 16, with seats and backs upholstered in rattan. An alternative seating arrangement to produce 35 seats was also considered. Luggage space would be provided at one end next to the driver's compartment. Westinghouse brakes would be provided and lighting was to be by acetylene gas. The vehicle would turn the scales at 12 tons unladen.

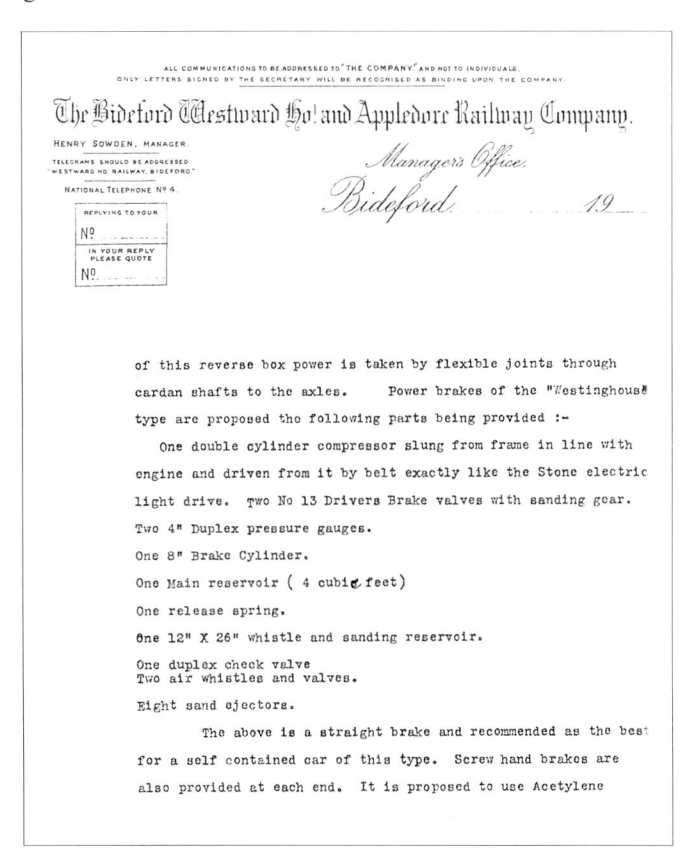

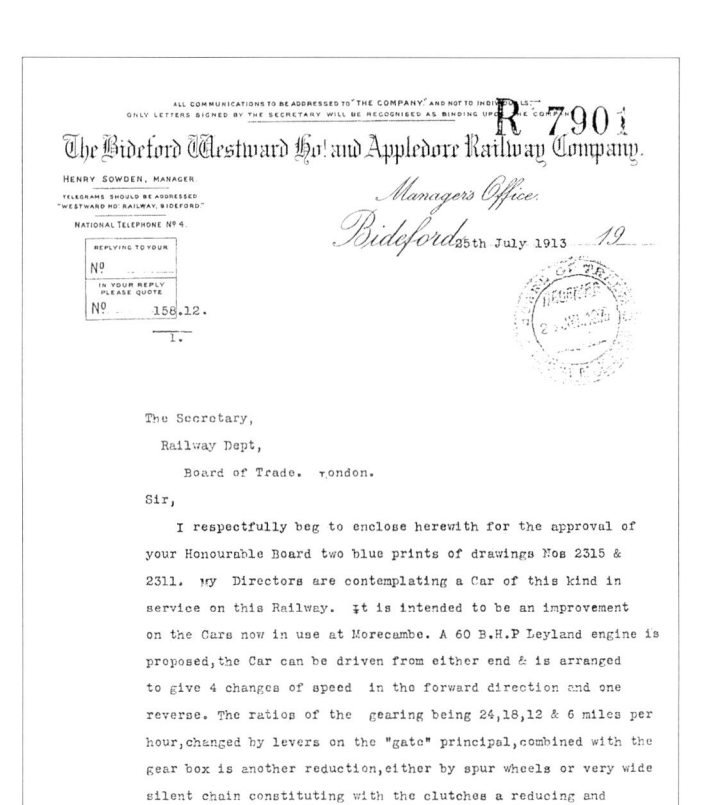

THE FINAL YEARS

A tranquil scene at Westward Ho! station in 1912. (Tom Bartlett Postcard Collection)

The Board of Trade were apparently reasonably happy with the proposals other than some alterations with respect of the siting of the petrol tank and the moving of the access steps. No further developments are recorded on this proposal and it is presumed that the outbreak of war ended the matter.

For some years before the Great War, the Devonshire Hussars Yeomanry spent a few weeks in camp at Westward Ho!, which generated small increase in traffic but had little effect on overall revenue.

At the Annual Meeting of the Railway Company held on 8th April 1914 it was noted that a loss of £1,661 11s 6d had been sustained for the year. Sadly, the meeting noted with regret the death of the good Captain Molesworth. Captain Molesworth was 89 years of age and been active virtually all his life; he was a great entrepreneur and his contribution to the local community and to the cause of railways cannot be overrated. It is comforting to know that he was spared the indignity of seeing "his" railway torn up.

War was declared on 4th August 1914 and shortly afterwards, the Railway Company received an official letter from the War Office dated "MIDNIGHT 4th/5th August 1914" and headed "SECRET".

The letter advised that under the provisions of the Regulation of the Forces Act 1871, the Company was taken over and placed in the hands of the Executive Committee of the Board of Trade! A further letter advised that compensation of £102 19s 4d would be payable. This action was later considered unnecessary and the takeover was rescinded as from 15th August 1914.

The war saw a slight increase in traffic for the line, with some troop movements early in the proceedings. The setting up of a Royal Naval Air Station at Westward Ho! also generated additional traffic. However, the line was hardly prosperous and in 1916 it was decided that the track and locomotives would be better employed assisting the supply effort on the front line in France. Accordingly, the line was requisitioned by the Government and the last train ran on 28th March 1917. Preparations were made for the locomotives to be sent off by rail and thus they had to be manoeuvred from the railway and on to the LSWR line at the goods station. Considerable work was carried out in laying temporary track from the end of the line on the Quay. There was not enough clearance to enable a curve to be laid directly onto the bridge and the track had to be curved round to the right and into Bridge Street. A point was laid off this line onto the bridge and the rest of the track laid up to the goods yard.

THE BIDEFORD, WESTWARD HO! & APPLEDORE RAILWAY

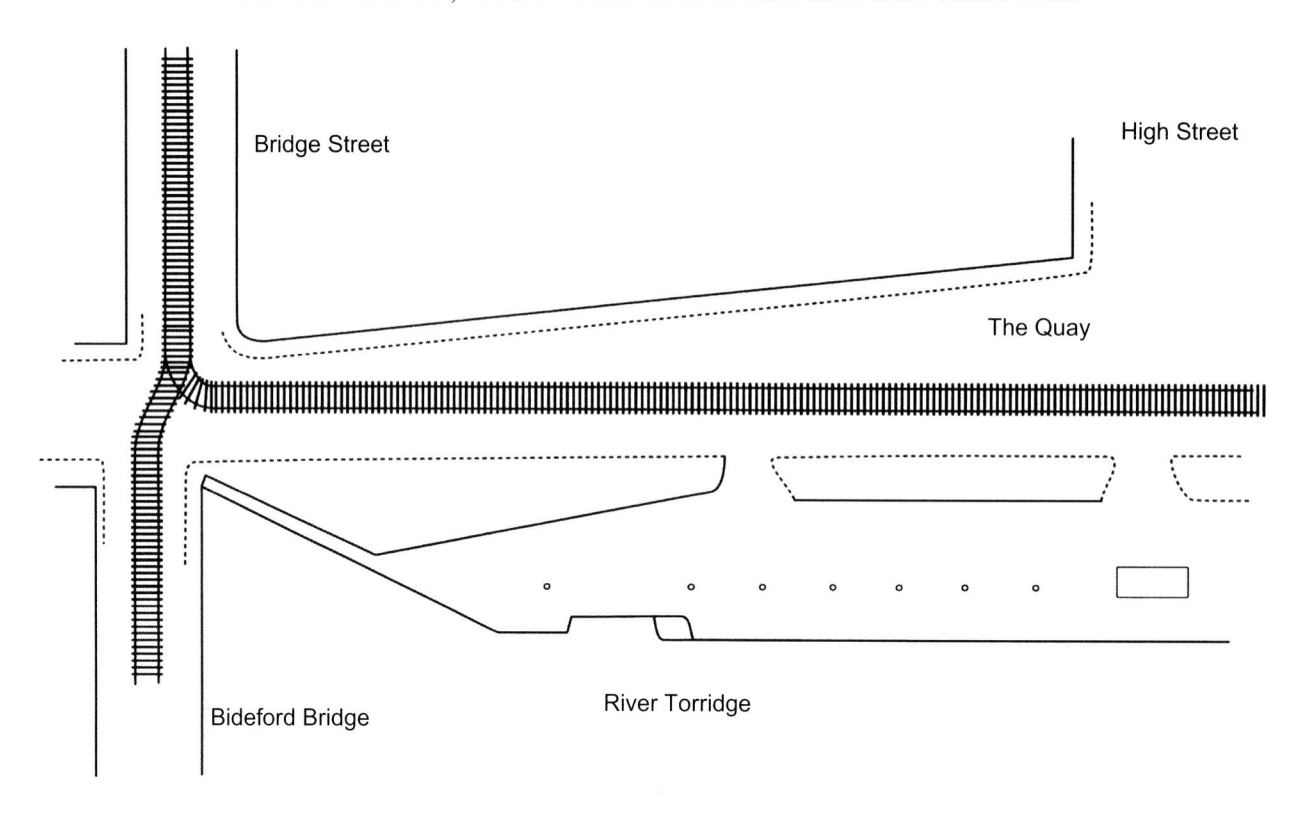

THE FINAL YEARS

On Sunday 29th July 1917 the folk of Bideford turned out in force to wave a fond (or in some cases not so fond) farewell to the little engines that had become part of the town over the previous sixteen years. They set off into Bridge Street and then, one by one steamed spiritedly off over the bridge. Their direction of travel had been altered by the shunt up Bridge Street, and working from a rare photograph of the engines in Bridge Street, *Grenville* and *Kingsley* must have gone over the bridge chimney first, whilst *Torridge* ran bunker first. They then spent the night in Barnstaple Street by the Royal Hotel, before running down to the goods yard on Monday morning.

It is interesting to compare the engines method of departure from Bideford with their arrival. It was noted earlier that, the Bridge Feoffees had insisted on the boilers being brought over the bridge separately from the rest of the locomotive to avoid strain on the bridge. It would seem that such efforts were unnecessary after all! The story of the little engines fate thereafter is clouded in mystery. Reports indicate that *Kingsley* went to the MOD at Avonmouth and thence to the National Smelting Co Ltd at Avonmouth where

Above: Looking up Bridge Street as one of the locos – not "Torridge" – waits her turn to run down the hill and over the bridge to meet her fate. (Roger Griffiths Collection)

Opposite page, top: A sketch of the end of the bridge and the Quay showing the probable arrangement of the temporary track laid to allow the locomotives over the bridge. Whilst pointwork is shown, it is probable that this was not actually laid, but that track was first laid from the end of the existing line on the Quay and up Bridge Street. The three locomotives would then have run up into Bridge Street. The Bridge Street track would then have been connected up with that already laid on the bridge and the locomotives steamed off over the bridge. (Martin Dowding)

Opposite page, bottom: Two locomotives backed up in Bridge Street before setting off over the bridge. It appears that one has already gone and the front engine is either "Grenville" or "Kingsley", with "Torridge" behind.
(Rob Dark Collection)

THE BIDEFORD, WESTWARD HO! & APPLEDORE RAILWAY

"Grenville" or "Kingsley" sets off over the bridge. (Bideford Library)

"Grenville" or "Kingsley" steams spiritedly away. (Chris Leigh Collection)

THE FINAL YEARS

she worked until 1937 when she was scrapped. The fate of *Grenville* and *Torridge* however is much less clear. It is alleged that from Bideford they went to Pembrey in Carmarthenshire and from there they found themselves on board a ship ostensibly bound for France. The only supposedly clear indication we have is that they were lost in the Bristol Channel when their ship was torpedoed.

Some or all of the signalling system was reputedly purchased by Colonel H.F. Stephens, the railway entrepreneur. It was dismantled and used on the Colonel's Weston, Clevedon and Portishead Railway.

Whilst I was researching this work, I was fortunate enough to meet Mr William Unett of Northam who, at 97 years of age remembered the railway when it was operational, and was able to relate some personal experiences of the line. Mr Unett's grandfather bought No 3, Kipling Terrace in Westward Ho! in about 1900 for £75. The house was reportedly sold in 1925 for about £250. Mr Unett thinks that the house was used largely as a holiday home for the extended family. If the weather was not good enough for the beach when they were staying there Mr Unett's father would take him on a round trip excursion. They would walk to the station at Westward Ho! and catch the train to Appledore. Another short walk to the quay and then they boarded the little ferry for a trip across the river to Instow. There they caught the "big" train to Bideford. Yet another walk, this time across the bridge, brought them to the BWHA station and a train ride back to Westward Ho! During WWI there was an aerodrome on the Burrows and Mr Unett used to watch the planes from Kipling Terrace. He remembers an incident one very misty day when a plane landed alongside the Pebble Ridge. It was fortunate that the tide was out as he had landed on the beach on the wrong side of the Pebble Ridge! After the closure of the line, Mr Unett and his friends used to play in the old inspection pit in the locomotive sheds, often being chased off by unknown adults!

The track was taken up soon after closure and presumably sent off to the war effort – possibly on the same ship as the engines. What happened to the goods wagons is not known, but the carriages were locked in the sheds at Bideford until after the War and then in 1921 they were auctioned off at 2.30pm on 20th April in the works yard by R. Blackmore & Sons of Bideford. Some of the track bed was held by B.E.T. until around 1928 before being sold off. Some of the carriages were evidently cut into sections after sale and were used as farm stores and the like. One half is known to still exist in a Bideford garden and hopefully this may yet be rescued and at least partially restored.

The track bed from the end of the Quay up past the locomotive and carriage sheds was made into part of the local road network as Kingsley Road. A similar exercise was undertaken at the other end of the line where Torridge Road

BIDEFORD, NORTH DEVON.

SIX LARGE MODERN BOGIE-WHEEL

Railway Coaches:

Clearance Sale of the Bideford, Westward Ho! and Appledore Railway Saloon Coaches.

R. Blackmore & Sons

Have received instructions to Sell by Auction as above, on

Wednesday, 20th April, 1921

At 2-30 p.m.

Auction and Estate Offices, Bideford, N. Devon.

The cover of the sale document for the six coaches. (Felton Vowler)

was built on the route of the line from Appledore station to Richmond Road Halt. Appledore station buildings were demolished although part of the back wall of the buildings still remains to this day; a recently erected large terracotta display replacing the small plaque which adorned the wall for many years. Westward Ho! station has gradually disappeared over the years and it is now difficult to see where the line once ran. The carriage and locomotive sheds at Bideford remained in other ownerships, but tragically the latter (a grade II listed building) was wantonly razed to the ground only a few years ago to be replaced by a used car dealership. Gradually nature reclaimed other parts of the route and most of the line is back in private ownership, although the section from Cornborough Cliffs into Westward Ho! is still a popular

105

PARTICULARS

Lot 1. ONE COACH, built by the Bristol Carriage Company, comprising: length, 48-ft.; width, 8-ft.; Four-wheel Bogies at each end; Standard Guage; Oil Boxes; Teak-wood Bodies; Walkover Seats, upholstered; One First-class Compartment, upholstered in leather; Platform at each end; lighted with Acetylene Gas; Vacuum Brakes; Seating capacity 10 first-class, 32 third-class.

Lot 2. ONE COACH similar to Lot 1.

Lot 3. ONE COACH similar to Lot 1.

Lot 4. ONE COACH similar to Lot 1.

Lot 5. ONE COACH comprising: length, 66-ft.; width, 8-ft.; Steel Underframes; Four-wheel Bogies at each end; Standard Guage; Oil Boxes; Oak Walkover Seats with Metal Supports; Platform at each end; lighted with Acetylene Gas; Vacuum Brakes; Seating capacity, 84, all third-class.

Lot 6. ONE COACH similar to Lot 5.

All Wheels 3-ft. diameter on tread.

Tyres, 2-in. thick.

Journals, 8 by 4½.

All the Coaches are in excellent condition.

The B. W. H. & A. Railway Company will allow reasonable time for removal, provided that the work is done without delay, and that the Railway Company are indemnified against any damage to their property.

The inside of the sale document for the six coaches with details of the lots. (Felton Vowler)

walk. A 1956 scheme to build a narrow gauge or miniature railway over part of the track bed came to nothing.

It is interesting to conjecture as to what might have been had circumstances been different. Certainly if the local Council had taken a less antagonistic attitude and worked with the railway company the fortunes of the line might have been better.

A more realistic timetable with marketing directed at potential passengers travelling to and from work earlier and later in the day might well have increased traffic to a more economic level. But isolated as it was from the rest of the network and running through the main street of the town it would have been surprising if the line had survived even without the intervention of the Great War. How different things might have been if the plans of George Molesworth and his partners had come to fruition. A branch off the LSWR line crossing the river by a new bridge and running out to Westward Ho! and Appledore with another branch to Clovelly and Hartland would have proved a much more viable option at the time. Through trains, or at least timed connections at the same station, would have brought more traffic and opened up the north coast for development. It would have made for a very interesting and delightful journey along the beautiful North Devon coastline. But situated in such an isolated location it would have probably gone the way of most such lines and succumbed to the Beeching axe.

Finally, "the tale of two engines" continues to reappear from time to time, and recently a shipwreck off the coast near Clovelly was found to contain the remains of what appear to be two standard gauge tank engines…

THE FINAL YEARS

The old crossing keeper's cottage on the Causeway from the road, some time after closure. The crossing gates are still in evidence. (Bideford Library)

The track of the railway looking away from Westward Ho! towards Seafield House in the centre background. Cornborough Cliffs are in the distance on the left. (Beaford Archive)

Part of one the coaches being used as a grain store on a local farm. (Marilyn Hughes, Westward Ho! History Group)

Another section of old coach disappearing into the undergrowth in a local garden. (Chris Leigh Collection)

The old Carriage shed on what is now Kingsley Road, Bideford. At the time of writing, this is still standing and in use as a motor coach garage. (Chris Leigh Collection)

THE FINAL YEARS

Top: The old engine shed just along from the carriage shed. Tragically, and unbelievably, this listed building was razed to the ground overnight only a few years ago to be replaced with a used car dealership. (Chris Leigh Collection)

Above, left: Allegedly the old signal box in use as a shop at Westward Ho! some years ago. It has now gone. (Marilyn Hughes, Westward Ho! History Group)

Above, right: The old station buildings at Westward Ho! hosting diesel engine powered buses. (Clive Fairchild Collection)

Left: The end of Station Hall at Westward Ho! with the track-bed now a road. (Marilyn Hughes, Westward Ho! History Group)

THE BIDEFORD, WESTWARD HO! & APPLEDORE RAILWAY

An undated shot of Bideford Quay which is believed to be after the railway closed. (Beaford Archive)

Looking down the Quay towards the Kingsley stature, probably some time after World War I. (Bideford Library)

Appendix A
The Bideford, Clovelly & Hartland Proposals

Sometime after June 1901, when the Bideford & Clovelly was abandoned, an application was made under the Light Railways Act of 1896 by the Western Counties Light Railway Company Ltd, a part of the B.E.T. group, for a railway starting with a junction with the Torrington Extension Railway near the tunnel at Landcross, to be known as The Bideford, Clovelly & Hartland Railway. The Torrington line at this point was running up the west bank of the Torridge, just before it crossed the river for the last time prior to reaching Bideford, and the new line was to continue along the west bank of the river up towards Bideford, and thence across country passing near Clovelly and entering Hartland between Natcott Lane and South Lane. A further line would run from the end of the new line back over the Torridge to join up with the LSWR at Bideford station. This latter section of the proposal was a contingency plan should the LSWR not agree to the connection at Landcross.

The Directors of the line were to be William Geoffrey Pine-Coffin, William Price Skinner and three others to be nominated by them. Captain G.M.F. Molesworth and George J. Taylor are mentioned in the first Light Railway Order, but not the later one. The line was to be of 4ft 8½in gauge with steam or other approved motive power, but not electric power. This is an interesting statement in view of the nature of the promoters' business. The engineer for the line was William Theodore Foxlee and he estimated the total cost of the line at £143,391 7s 3d. As well as the connection to the LSWR line at Landcross, there was to be further work at Bideford station to accommodate additional traffic. This latter involved widening the station and plans were actually drawn up at Waterloo for the work.

On 7th February 1905, a large gathering met in the Bridge Hall, Bideford, in support of the proposed new railway and to hear the details of the route and costs from Mr. Foxlee, the Engineer. The meeting was enthusiastic in its support and the majority of those present signed a petition of support.

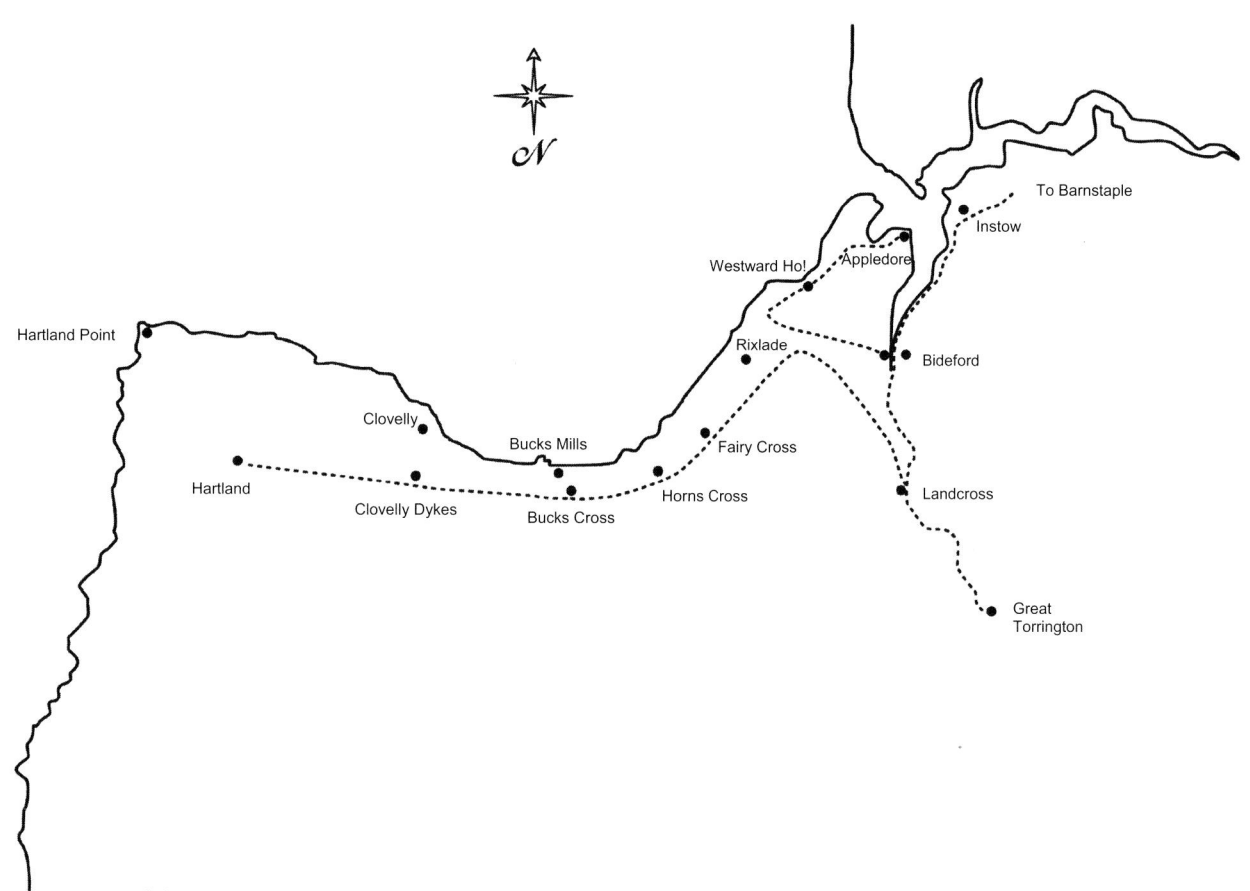

Map of the route of the proposed Bideford Clovelly and Hartland Railway. (Martin Dowding)

THE BIDEFORD, WESTWARD HO! & APPLEDORE RAILWAY

At a hearing in Bideford before the Light Railway Commissioners on 29th March 1905, another larger and enthusiastic meeting largely backed the proposals. Major Paton of Foxdown wished to know if the trees in his garden would be avoided. Mr Foxlee gave such an assurance! The LSWR voiced its approval of the scheme and support from merchants, traders and landowners was also heard. The Commissioners were satisfied with the proposals and agreed to grant the Order. In June meetings were held in Hartland and Clovelly to gain positive support and committees were elected to canvass financial support in the area.

The Bill passed the necessary scrutiny and the Bideford, Clovelly & Hartland Light Railway Order was issued in 1905, with a modified version appearing in 1906.

Conditions were incorporated into the proposals regarding protection of certain landowners' interests. These stipulated that no deviation could be made onto their land outside the agreed lines on the plans. Specific mention of two landowners is made in the 1905 Order, but only a general mention appears in the 1906 version.

In spite of the apparent support locally, it proved difficult to obtain the necessary finance for the line and, as was often the case with such schemes, little was done to proceed with the work. Agreements regarding deviations also proved difficult and as late as 21st May 1913, Foxlee was writing to the government seeking funding assistance for the scheme. The LSWR had agreed to work the line and a further letter on 27th June 1913 from Foxlee to the Board of Trade sets out the arrangements. The LSWR would take 60% of the revenue and the BCH the remaining 40%, subject to a 4% dividend being earned by the BCH. If this was not the case the LSWR were to give a rebate from their 60%. The same letter also advises a reduction in the estimate for the main part of the line from Landcross to Hartland from £111,131 6s 4d to £106,850 which included a 10% contingency provision. Also the proposals for widening at Bideford were dropped, and the onset of war in 1914 no doubt ensured that the whole scheme forever remained only a proposal.

BIDEFORD, CLOVELLY, AND HARTLAND LIGHT RAILWAY.

ESTIMATE OF EXPENSE.

SUMMARY.

	Length. M. F. C.	Cost. £ s. d.
Railway No. 1	13　0　5·80	108,567　2　0
Railway No. 2	0　2　0·55	2,564　4　4
Railway No. 3	1　7　2·35	32,101　3　6
Railway No. 4	0　0　3·00	158　17　5
Total length	15　2　1·70	Total cost £143,391　7　3

The engineer's estimate of expenses for the construction of the line in November 1901.

Appendix B
Accidents and Incidents

There are few reports of accidents during the railway's short life, but the first recorded occurred on 18th October 1901 when a coach became derailed near the Baths at Westward Ho! Contemporary reports state that "the permanent way was torn up and the carriages smashed, but no one was hurt". No other details are known and it is suspected that the incident was relatively minor.

On 26th September 1902 an incident with a horse took place on the Quay whilst one of the engines was apparently shunting some goods wagons on the Quay. The *North Devon Journal* reported: "...a spirited animal was being driven along the road attached to a dog cart. The animal reared at the engine and overturned the cart, the driver the only occupant being thrown out. He was not hurt."

In August 1904, a Bideford Town Councillor was summonsed for using foul and abusive language on a train to the annoyance of other passengers. He was fined 30s with 13s costs.

On Sunday, 4th August 1907, John Loughlin, the stationmaster at Westward Ho! was concerned to see three young men who appeared to be fighting and using bad language on the station platform. As there were other passengers on the platform and a train was approaching, he asked them to stop. One of the men however caught him round the neck and punched him on both sides of the face with his fists. The Company were anxious to set an example and the man was arraigned before Bideford County Magistrates. The man pleaded guilty and was fined 10s with 7s 6d costs. The Chairman of the bench remarked to the defendant "you are lucky to get off so cheaply".

The end of August 1910 saw "an alarming incident, in which a motor-cyclist had an almost miraculous escape from sudden death" on 26th August 1910. The motor cyclist was driving down the Pill "at quite a moderate speed" his view being restricted by the Art School on his right and a hedge on the left. A gateway on the corner, which was usually closed, was open, and the motor-cyclist headed towards this gap. Two ladies walking along were about to cross in front of the gateway when they saw the motorcycle and stepped back. The cyclist came on and at that point the 4.35pm from Bideford to Appledore hove into view. The driver, seeing the motorcycle heading straight for him, applied the brakes and succeeded in stopping the train in less than its own length. The ladies being on the motorcyclist's left, the rider turned slightly to the right to avoid them but hit the cowcatcher on the front of the locomotive. He was thrown off his machine and sustained minor injuries – his cycle suffered rather more. The newspaper report praised the engine driver for his prompt action and the design of cowcatcher which prevented the rider from going under the train.

On an unknown date the driver of a train having just returned to Bideford found blood splashed over the front of his locomotive. *Kingsley* had worked to Westward Ho! and back and there was no indication as to the source of the blood other than some fur. On the next down trip the mangled remains of a donkey were found by the side of the line near Abbotsham Road station. The owner was traced and paid compensation for the loss of the beast.

Appendix C
The Railway Inspectorate

Whilst the early development of railways was largely free from government control – other than such control as Parliament had over Bills for new railways – it was felt that some form of oversight was required. The Board of Trade at that time was responsible for overseas trade and shipping but had no involvement with inland transport. Parliament eventually decided that the Board should have an involvement and in 1840 set up the Railway Department of the Board of Trade with a remit to inspect new lines and certify they were fit for public opening. It was also empowered to investigate railway accidents and to report, with recommendations, thereon. Railway Companies were also obliged to submit annual returns of traffic to the Department.

The staff of the new Department knew nothing of the mechanics of railway construction or operation and its inspectors were therefore drawn from officers of the Royal Engineers. Whilst they were highly qualified men in their own fields, they had to learn the specifics of railways largely from their own, and colleagues, experience collected "on the job". That said they soon proved to be highly competent and well respected in their job and were instrumental in bringing about many of the safety features of railways that still exist today, such as the interlocking of points and signals and the fitting of the continuous automatic brake to all trains. Experience in investigating accidents enabled them to foresee potential problems with new lines and to have alterations and improvements made before new lines opened.

The two inspectors who were involved with the Bideford, Westward Ho! & Appledore, Lt-Colonel H.A. Yorke and Major J.W. Pringle, were both held in high esteem in their profession. Major Pringle went on to serve in World War I as a full Colonel in the role of Deputy Director of Railway Transport, ranking as Assistant Adjutant General. After the war he returned to the Railway Department, investigating such accidents as the dreadful single line collision at Abermule in 1921, the River class locomotive derailment at Sevenoaks in 1927, and the horrific Charfield accident in 1928. He was later made a Companion of the Order of the Bath (C.B.) and knighted for his services.

Also available from Kestrel Railway Books

The Torrington & Marland Light Railway by Rod Garner

Set in rural North Devon, the Torrington & Marland Light Railway was developed to move products from the Marland Brick and Clay Company's works at Peters Marland to the LSWR railhead at Torrington station for onward distribution to Barnstaple and beyond.

Devon is a county rich in industrial history, and a full account of this, one of the best known of its narrow gauge clay lines, is long overdue. Author, Rod Garner has amassed a vast amount of material on the railway and on the clay works that were the reason for its existence, much of it seen here for the first time.

Renowned for its wooden viaducts and trestles, in addition to its unusual motive-power, the Torrington and Marland Light Railway has now passed into history, but in this book it is resurrected for anyone who was not fortunate to see it in its heyday.

ISBN 978-0-9544859-7-9
£14.00